TODAY'S CHUCKLE

2500

Great
One-Liners

FOR EVERY OCCASION

Paul Harlan Collins

A Perigee Book

I dedicate this book to my mom, Beulah, who, realizing the enormity of it all, chose to laugh.

Perigee Books
are published by
The Putnam Publishing Group
200 Madison Avenue
New York, NY 10016

Library of Congress Cataloging-in-Publication Data

Collins, Paul Harlan.
   Today's chuckle : 2500 great one-liners for every occasion / Paul
Harlan Collins.
      p. cm.
   ISBN 0-399-51810-X
   1. American wit and humor.   I. Title.   II. Title: 2500 great one-liners for
every occasion.   III. Title: Twenty-five hundred great one-liners for every occasion.
PN6162.C653   1993   92-46602 CIP
818′.5402–dc20

Book design by H. Roberts
Cover design by Paul Perlow
Cover illustration © by Lisa Goldrick

Printed in the United States of America
1   2   3   4   5   6   7   8   9   10

ACKNOWLEDGMENTS

When Sir Isaac Newton was asked what inspired his discoveries, he replied, "I have stood on the shoulders of giants."

I have at least sat in the laps of the giants of humor, and then they stood up.

CONTENTS

Affairs of State and Other Political Indiscretions:
Why are politicians like polkas? They have different
names, but they all sound alike.   7

Crazy for You:
Why Noah's Ark was probably the last cruise ship with
enough males to go around.   24

Marriage, Divorce, and Beyond:
Why some folks think that marriage gives you a new
leash on life.   28

Keep It in the Family:
Wouldn't it be great if all children behaved like you
think you did when you were a kid?   34

In Sickness and in Health:
Let's hope our doctors' medical techniques are more
up-to-date than the magazines in their waiting rooms.   44

Of Sound Mind and Body:
You shouldn't let people drive you crazy when you
know it's only walking distance.   49

All Is Vanity:
A compliment is like mouthwash: it feels great but
sometimes it's tough to swallow.   59

You Know You're Getting Old When . . . :
The best way to stay young is eat right, exercise, and
lie about your age.   62

Spiritual Truths:
Nothing makes it easier to resist temptation than a
strong moral upbringing—and witnesses. 68

Show Biz:
It took about fifty years for movies to go from silent to
unspeakable. 73

Wonders of Science:
Evolution is nature's way of covering its mistakes. 78

Legal Liabilities:
Never hire a lawyer who has the courage of
your convictions. 83

Real Jobs:
You don't truly know what job security is until you're
right-hand man to a guy named Lefty. 85

The Getting of Wisdom:
Just when you think you know the meaning of the
word "stupid," someone comes along and redefines it. 95

The Sporting Life:
The next time someone tells you nothing is impossible,
ask him to dribble a football. 98

In the Spirit of the Season:
There are two kinds of Christmas gifts: those you
don't like, and those you don't get. 102

Art for Art's Sake:
When someone is said to have an artistic
temperament, it means they're too old to spank. 104

Stormy Weather:
Some people are like snow: they storm in
and act like flakes. 107

Nature Calls:
The real reason dogs are man's best friend is that they
·don't understand a word you're saying.   109

The Social Order:
No matter how small a town is, you can always find
someone to give you wrong directions.   114

Creature Comforts:
When couch potatoes pause on the educational TV
channel, they have a near-depth experience.   127

High Finance:
Asking a stockbroker if you should invest in the
market is like asking a dog if it's hungry.   132

Money and the Meaning of Life:
Prosperity is that period between the last installment
and the next purchase.   137

Life's Instructions:
Never be nostalgic about anything unless there's
absolutely no chance of its coming back again.   147

The Last Word:
The End.   159

AFFAIRS OF STATE AND OTHER POLITICAL INDISCRETIONS

Diplomat: someone who thinks twice before saying nothing.

The concept of taxation is simple: you can shear a sheep repeatedly, but you can only skin it once.

Disarmament: agreement between nations to dismantle all the weapons that are obsolete anyway.

Many politicians leave office because of illness and fatigue . . . people are sick and tired of them.

What's the big deal about George Washington's throwing a dollar across the Potomac? Congress throws millions of them over the ocean every day.

We'd have better environmental legislation if special-interest groups were biodegradable.

Politics is a field full of promise . . . politicians keep making one promise after another.

Maybe there should be a politicians' obedience school—for those who renege on campaign promises.

We, as a country, have always owed a great debt to our forefathers. Now we owe a great debt to everybody.

Scientists have just discovered that the greenhouse effect has radically worsened due to all the politicians' blowing nothing but hot air about the environment.

Why is it that when politicians clean house, they end up sweeping things under the rug?

Certain politicians have perfected the latest exercise craze: aerobic lying.

Who says nothing ever changes? Washington never told a lie, and now the guys in Washington never tell the truth.

The wheels of justice may grind slowly, but in some countries justice more closely resembles a food processor.

The ship of state would be better off if there weren't so many pirates on board.

I don't know about politicians' having any intuitive powers, but they are certainly good at forestalling the future.

Political parties are just like any other kind of party: they hand out favors and drink too much.

Government contractors like to put their best foot forward with congressmen. That way they're in the right position to give kickbacks.

If you think the Cold War is over, just wait until you see appliance manufacturers battling it out to sell new refrigerators to Eastern Europe.

It's all very well for congressmen to stand for the red, white, and blue, but why do so many have to lie for the green?

Everyone talks about keeping lit the eternal flame of freedom, but nobody wants to pay the gas bill.

If you're really seeking higher office, become a lighthouse keeper.

Urban crime is getting so bad that, instead of handing out keys to the city, they hand out lockpicks.

Congress: where our elected officials catch naps between meetings with lobbyists.

Politicians have a lot of drive . . . that's why they keep shifting positions.

The problem with modern leaders isn't that they don't speak their minds . . . it's just so little to speak of.

Politicians used to get caught with their hands in the cookie jar. Now they just take the whole bakery.

Bullfighter: congressional watchdog.

Some congressmen would like to scrap the Bill of Rights and institute the Bill of Write-offs.

These are the times that try men's souls . . . and if the government has anything to say about it, it'll be the time to tax men's souls, too.

It's not surprising to see so many politicians standing on their heads to get votes . . . it's the only way to put your foot down if it's in your mouth.

A politician will always try to put more fire in his rhetoric . . . unless he's scared of making an ash of himself.

There are two ways for ex-presidents to test their popularity: publish their memoirs and run for dogcatcher.

Americans may not like burning the flag, but they don't mind if it sparks controversy and takes a little heat.

The whole country's jumping out of the frying pan and into the microwave.

Of all the taxes the government imposes, the worst is the tax on our patience.

Politicians like to air their differences . . . that's why so many of them are windbags.

If politics isn't for the birds, why are all those politicians always parroting the same old lines?

Maybe those politicians should appropriate some money for a washing machine, with all that dirty laundry they're airing.

Then there was the alien emissary who was so short he said, "Take me to your ladder."

It can ruin a kid's future to get a police record . . . then he couldn't run for Congress and become a big-time crook.

Too many congressmen start out running for election and end up running from the ethics committee.

If an elephant never forgets, how come the Republicans keep making the same mistakes?

If Samson slew his enemies with the jawbone of an ass, why can't the Democrats do better with all those jawbones of the donkey?

They say laughter makes the world go 'round . . . and there are sure plenty of clowns running it.

Maybe more politicians would have ethics if they knew where to buy them.

Steamy novel: one that's full of hot air and fiction . . . like the memoirs of a politician.

If amnesia isn't contagious, how come all those politicians always forget their campaign promises as soon as they get together in Congress?

Those guys at the Pentagon are just like school kids . . . all they want is a little launch money.

Lesson to dictators: into every life some reign must fall.

If we don't solve the energy crisis, the sheikh will inherit the earth.

The government ought to appoint a Secretary of Barbers, considering all the close shaves it gets us into.

Worst guy to have in a nuclear-missile silo: someone with a button-down mind.

If governments are supposed to orchestrate the affairs of the country, then congressmen must be the wind instruments.

Gross national product: a federal fertilizer factory.

You can't fool all of the people all of the time . . . but politicians are satisfied with fifty-one percent.

The one dessert they don't serve in the Senate cafeteria: humble pie.

Politicians ought to learn the difference between showing horse sense and being stubborn as a mule.

When politicians see the writing on the wall, they whitewash it.

Maybe we wouldn't have to worry so much about congressional pork barrels if there weren't so many swine in Washington.

If only we could get our politicians to learn to sit and heel. All they can do now is roll over.

There are plenty of UFOs in Washington: unprincipled federal officials.

If our congressmen had more horse sense, maybe we'd have a more stable government.

Congress passes plenty of laws that have teeth to them . . . the problem is, they're dentures.

Taxpayers are suggesting a new mode of dress and transportation for some congressmen: tar and feathers and a rail.

History teaches us to make the same mistakes with a sense of tradition.

Here's a great new way to spend taxpayers' money: a government study on stress reduction for sloths.

Lots of people save something for a rainy day, but politicians have slush funds.

Politics may be for the birds, but all the birds are vultures.

The reason our politicians have such far-reaching vision is that hot air makes you rise.

If this country is going to the dogs, at least this administration will make sure it's the right pedigree.

Once upon a time, we had leaders with a vision. Now we have them with evasion.

What have people got against video dating? After all, it's the same way we pick our presidents.

Political embarrassment: when you throw your hat into the ring, and everyone realizes it's just a beanie.

It's a short distance between politically correct and politically corrupt.

If we really wanted a president experienced in counterintelligence, we could have elected a short-order cook.

If there's no rest for the wicked, then what are all those deposed dictators doing at the resort spots?

The reason folks like a brass band on the podium at political rallies is so they can take the bull by the horns.

Maybe we should elect a matador president; then we'd have somebody qualified to deal with all the bull from Congress.

Don't worry about losing weight. If the government helps the farmer any more, we'll all be on diets.

Our leaders promise us the nation is shipshape. The problem is, the ship they're referring to is the *Lusitania*.

Foresight: what our politicians exhibit . . . but only on the golf course.

Everybody makes mistakes. If you make enough of them, you can become president.

IRS: income removal service.

Evolution tells us that we came from monkeys, but they didn't tell us we were going to turn into donkeys and elephants.

The reason so many people run for public office is that they know they can lie down on the job as soon as they get it.

This country has come a long way: from our forefathers to the four-flushers.

It's not the ship of state that's in trouble . . . it's the rubber ducky of diplomacy.

Life is largely semantics. For example, bank robbers steal money, politicians appropriate it.

If only they'd make a combination voting booth/vending machine, then we could at least get something out of it.

Government should take more interest in exploring space . . . particularly between politicians' ears.

New politics: that's the same old song and dance, but with new arrangements.

Politicians live a dog's life . . . like a French poodle.

Next time Congress tries to pull a rabbit out of a hat, remember that the rabbit is cousin to the rat.

The Democrat Party symbol might be apt, but you never saw a donkey making a Democrat out of himself.

You would think the ship of state would move quicker, what with all those bags of wind in Congress.

What this country needs is a president who can speak his mind . . . in complete sentences.

Those people in Congress are really into advanced math when they tackle the budget. They only know how to deal with negative numbers.

If politicians think TV coverage is so important, why do they keep giving us reruns?

Not all things are etched in stone . . . the things our politicians tell us, for instance, are etched in mud.

A politician is someone who follows public opinion and then calls himself a leader.

Don't talk about things you know nothing about. People might think you're running for office.

If silence is golden, no wonder those windbags in Congress took us off the gold standard.

When Congress enacts a law, you can be sure it'll really have some gums to it.

Even the Republicans are tightening their belts this year . . . the only problem is, they're ermine belts.

Isn't it time somebody stood up to the president and said, "Are you a man, or are you a mouth?"

New punishment for government officials convicted of crimes: instead of sending them to prisons like country clubs, they simply confine them to their own country clubs.

A politician is someone who shows you a mirage in the desert and then tries to sell you a drinking cup.

A political pundit is someone who draws your own conclusions.

Not too many candidates are running for president, but there are quite a few limping for the office.

President: someone who sleeps in the White House, acts like a white knight, and knows how to whitewash.

Be kind to our friends, the birds. After all, they're on a brain-exchange program with many of our top government officials.

Mrs. Washington may have given us the father of our country, but it's Mrs. Cow who gives us the fodder of our country.

We don't mind a politician with his hand in the cookie jar once in a while
. . . but we draw the line when he takes all the dough and gets a kickback
from the jar manufacturer.

In politics, the issue is not so much what the candidate stands for as what
the voters will fall for.

Politicians are like steers: they make a couple of good points off the top of
their head, and the rest is all bull.

A successful politician knows how to deliver the goods before he gets caught
with them.

Some politicians leave their footprints on the sands of time; others leave their
fingerprints on the scams of slime.

Political entomology: the study of bugging politicians' offices.

It's not whether you win or lose . . . it's how you stuff the ballot box.

Some countries have an open-door policy . . . but many more have an
open-hand policy.

Who needs TV? We get plenty of bad old jokes and bad writing from
presidential candidates.

It's hard for the presidential candidates to pick running mates. They have to
find someone who will fill their shoes without stepping on their toes.

If George Washington were alive today and still refused to tell a lie, he
wouldn't even get elected mayor.

Air bags in cars: when politicians drive.

If ignorance is bliss, Congress must be the happiest place on earth.

Washington plastic surgeons offer a two-for-one price for face-lifts to
politicians . . . makes it economical for those who are two-faced.

There seems to be a rule for government officials who abuse power: break the
law, join the lecture circuit.

They ought to open a congressional kissing booth. All they're good at is lip
service anyway.

If you really want to go into politics, get married.

If there's such a thing as word pollution, then Congress must be a toxic
dump site.

Some politicians who toss their hat into the ring leave their head in it.

Maybe money won't buy happiness, but it'll buy you a seat in the U.S. Senate.

If you can't teach an old dog new tricks, why are congressmen always coming up with fresh scandals?

Most politicians lead a foot-to-mouth existence.

If we're going to elect actors to political office, don't you think we should get ones who can remember their lines?

If this country is going to the dogs, then how come all the fat cats are doing so well?

Most presidents have a nodding acquaintance with the law . . . when someone brings up the law, they start to nod off.

If you really want a scary costume next Halloween, dress up as a congressman.

Paying taxes to the government is feeding the hand that bites you.

People accuse Congress of dragging its feet on legislation, but in reality they're right on schedule. Problem is, it's an airline schedule.

Our congressmen really know how to handle money. When they're not passing the buck, they're pocketing it.

They're adding a new Olympic event for White House press secretaries: verbal gymnastics.

What's so bad about the world going to the dogs? At least we'll get plenty of naps.

Scientists claim some people are right-brained and others left-brained. Politicians claim that they are right-brained and opponents are left-without-a-brain.

When parliamentarians dance on the furniture, they call it tabling the motion.

He who laughs last just got the government contract for thousand-dollar toilet seats.

If crime doesn't pay, how come so many people run for political office?

If Congress planned our recreational activities as they do the budget, we'd be waterskiing behind canoes.

You can't call our politicians cheap crooks . . . not at the prices they charge.

About the only way for crime not to pay is to nationalize it.

Politician: someone who puts his best foot forward . . . into his mouth.

It's too bad the Constitution doesn't include the right to bear alms.

How come every time one of these Washington guys is touched by scandal, the rest of the country is beat up by it?

It seems as if the only way to get elected now is if you have friends in low places.

Lame-duck presidents have a doglike devotion to the electorate . . . they roll over and play dead.

Political archaeology: the study of how someone can be above suspicion and still be beneath contempt.

Politician: someone who shakes your hand before the election and your confidence after.

Congress: where the exchange of ideas meets the exchange of ideals and you end up making deals.

The cannibals know how to treat their heads of state. They let them remain heads, but that's all.

As they say on Capitol Hill, love is where you fund it.

Honest politician: one who will live up to his promise after being bribed only once.

It's a short distance from being a smooth politician to being a slippery crook.

Every time a politician works up a head of steam, hot air comes out of his mouth.

The main reason that politicians champion free speech in this country is that they're not going to listen to what we say anyway.

Presidential elections always bring out the beast in the candidates.

Just because the government is trying to save money is no reason to elect two-bit politicians.

Every time we elect a president who will just dance to our tune, he does the sidestep.

When candidates are discovered in romantic trysts, it's known as skirting the issue.

These days the ship of state seems to carry only one cargo: pork barrels.

A politician is someone who will do almost anything to get a crowd's attention. So is a clown.

Some say a political race is like a horse race, but at least the horses are qualified to run.

Politician: someone who keeps the country on thin ice and expects us to pay for the skates.

An experienced politician knows how not to wince when making his own pronouncements.

Congressmen feel obligated to work for the greatest number . . . usually no less than five figures.

Conservative: someone with both feet planted firmly in cement.

What can you say about a government that expects us to pay taxes and then uses it to pay interest on all the money they borrowed?

People who refuse to face the facts usually end up getting elected president.

March isn't the only thing that comes in like a lion and goes out like a lamb. So do politicians.

They say ignorance is bliss, which must be the reason we keep voting the same guys into office.

Vice president: the lesser of two evils.

Politicians ought to learn basic arithmetic: the surest way to divide the country is to subtract from the taxpayers' income.

Politician: someone who stands up and rocks the boat, then blames it on the weather.

You can only believe half of what a politician tells you. The question is, which side of their mouth is telling the truth?

The real reason congressmen are trying to get reelected is that they know they couldn't find another job in this economy.

Lots of politicians have good, sound reasoning . . . their reasons always sound good.

When politicians get to the meat of the matter, it's usually baloney.

You'd think politicians would speak more sweetly, considering how often they have to eat their words.

Our leaders have to be ready to rise to the occasion . . . that's why they stay so full of hot air.

All politicians have strong opinions on the issues . . . they just keep them to themselves.

Presidential elections always get down to the character issue: which candidate is the biggest character.

Why do people complain about congressmen's expense accounts, and then complain about cheap politicians?

It's odd how many politicians throw the dirt from on top of a soapbox.

Since nothing's sure but death and taxes, Congress has decided to put a tax on dying.

Every four years the political parties push their most promising politicians. Those are the ones who make the most promises.

A politician is one who, generally speaking, is generally speaking.

Isn't it a shame that future generations won't be here to see all the wonderful things the government is doing with their money?

Maybe politicians who read tea leaves should wake up and smell the coffee instead.

Candidates always move to the center of the road as election day approaches. After all, they're only being fair to middling.

Our politicians spend so much time on shaky ground, maybe we should start grading them on the Richter scale.

For Washington lobbyists, the road to success is a toll road.

Our politicians know how to run the government. The problem is the ground they're running it into.

Wouldn't it be great if our politicians had guidance systems just half as sophisticated as our missiles?

Political campaigns appeal to our bitter nature.

Some of our politicians are getting so old that, instead of running for reelection, they'll be crawling for it.

If this country is going to the dogs, maybe it's because the congressmen haven't been to obedience school.

Some politicians are men of vision, and some politicians just have double vision.

Some of these politicians should take courses in remedial thinking.

Politicians are just like young people in love . . . they make promises they can't keep, and spend money on things they can't afford.

In a recent popularity poll, politicians scored slightly below airline chefs.

Politician: someone who shakes your hand before the election and has you shaking your head after they're in office.

Dirty politics: a redundancy.

Politicians wouldn't be able to do any mudslinging if they didn't dig up some dirt in the first place.

The day Democrats and Republicans can get along will probably be the same day that dogs and cats form a social club.

The reason the government can't find out what the average American wants is they can't find any Americans who think they're average.

If pro is the opposite of con, then progress is the opposite of congress.

Political speech: when all is said and dumb.

Lots of politicians are part of the back-to-nature movement . . . they constantly turn their backs on nature.

It's funny how all these presidential candidates keep looking for photo opportunities, only to turn out negative.

How can those congressmen have such swelled heads and be so small-minded at the same time?

It's tough being a politician. You never know when people have stopped following you and started chasing you.

I don't want to say the televised Senate sessions are boring, but most folks would prefer watching a PBS special on the garden slug.

Political campaign: when candidates air each other's dirty laundry and try to avoid static cling.

Now that the arms race is over, the Russians have devised a new one . . . the open hand.

Fireside chat: when the president gets on TV, acts warm, and fires you up before you get burned.

Disarmament is like a Hollywood party. Nobody wants to be the first to arrive.

The difference between a liberal and a conservative is whether they listen to new ideas with an open mind or an open mouth.

Our president is a man of many parts . . . but then, so was Frankenstein.

Why congressmen want to be committee chairmen: it's harder to see where they stand if they're always sitting down on the job.

Somebody should tell our politicians that having a swelled head is not the same thing as being broad-minded.

The people keep looking for someone of presidential timber, but so far the only timber is in the candidates' heads.

Presidential staff: the big stick they carry when they talk softly.

A lot of politicians claim they were farm boys. That's probably why they use a lot of corn and bull.

One look at Congress and you know some people are born leaders . . . and the rest just buy the position.

You can't fool all of the people all of the time . . . that's why we have the electoral college.

It's not to say that politicians oversimplify society's problems, but most of their explanations go right under your head.

America is becoming the biggest debtor nation on earth, and most Americans seem proud to be doing their part.

What good would it do to put a spending cap on Congress? They already spend plenty without wearing any headgear at all.

Maybe we should recruit our next president from Broadway . . . then he'd really know how to give us the old song and dance.

It's great the way Congress handles the federal budget. It's like writing a check and having the bank bounce.

Congressmen stand on their records . . . that's why they're always talking in circles.

If any more birdbrains get elected to Congress, we're going to have to tear down the House and Senate and replace them with aviaries.

When grizzlies run for public office: pander bear.

Most politicians keep in shape by straddling fences.

Entitlement programs: the money we give the government to give back to us, after handling charges.

Progressive: someone who wants things to stay exactly the same in innovative, exciting ways.

There's one good thing about ignorance: it keeps a lot of politicians employed.

A president is someone who casts the ship of state adrift at sea, and then blames the opposing party for forgetting the anchor.

Debating candidates try to prove they're presidential timber . . . that's why they give such wooden performances.

Government waste: any money not spent in your own state.

If a picture is worth a thousand words, why don't more campaigns end up in a draw?

Of course lots of politicians have narrow minds. What else would fit inside those pointed heads?

Some people would like to run this country like a business . . . and others think having one vice president is enough.

With the New World Order, we can now get in skirmishes with countries we never even heard of before.

If you really want to cut down on the defense budget, make the Pentagon sponsor fund-raising drives for their weapons.

Beware of a politician who offers a chicken in every pot. He's probably got other birdbrained ideas as well.

If we all learn from our mistakes, then politicians must be the best-educated people.

If George Washington never told a lie, he couldn't have had a lot of fishing buddies.

Every time our society is at a crossroads, we want a new crossing guard.

At least there's no danger of these politicians' taxing our imagination.

Politics would be an easy job if only taxpayers and voters weren't the same people.

The breakup of the Soviet Union sure helped one segment of the economy: mapmakers.

Scratch the surface of any politician and you'll just get more surface.

Sincerity is the most important thing politicians have to learn to fake.

George Washington didn't have to lie. He never had to pay income taxes.

Only one person in a million really understands the international situation. Isn't it odd how you keep running into him?

Modern politicians are well versed in the questions of the day. They just don't know the answers.

At least George Washington didn't blame his troubles on the previous administration.

Washington's problem is they have to dig the country out of the hole without making the hole any bigger.

Political campaigns are based on the premise that you can't try a man for blaming.

The cheapest way to have your family tree traced is to run for office.

There's never any point in trying to reason with someone who's drunk, in love, or running for office.

At least if you're a politician your wife never criticizes you in public.

Who says Congress spends money like drunken sailors? Sailors spend their own money.

Wouldn't it be great if politicians could get as much mileage out of our tax dollars as they do from an alphabet with only twenty-six letters?

No wonder presidents don't understand our economic woes: they get to veto their bills.

Conservative politician: one who would like to improve things just the way they are.

Politician: someone who's interested in wordy causes.

Spending more money to solve our country's ills seems a lot like trying to fill a bathtub with no stopper in the drain.

Politicians are like polkas. They have different names, but they all sound alike.

CRAZY FOR YOU

If there's such a thing as lovesickness, then a pretty girl is like a malady.

Engagement: that final period in which lovers keep up their pretenses.

Puppy love: prelude to a dog's life.

If you're burning with desire, make sure you don't make an ash out of yourself.

By the time you're old enough to understand the opposite sex, they don't notice you anymore.

When you bring out the beast in most men, it's a pig.

Most lovers find rivers romantic. It puts them in a sedimental mood.

Love is a two-way street. That's so you can be driven crazy coming and going.

If all the world loves a lover, how come there's a law against polygamy?

Dimestore Romeo: a wolf in cheap clothing.

Some couples love to bicker. For them, it was love at first spite.

Love is always colorful . . . you're either in the pink, seeing red, or feeling blue.

They say love is a two-way street, but nobody ever tells you about all the stop signs.

Did you hear about the two fingerprints who couldn't make love work because they were from two different whorls?

The problem with the game of love is they keep rewriting the rule book.

The problem with building a relationship is that too many people use a hammer in the construction.

There are plenty of other fish in the sea, but they're probably piranhas.

Show me a couple with high dental and manicure bills, and I'll show you a couple who's always fighting tooth and nail.

When to break your date with a guy: when he refers to you as "the catch of the day."

You know your social life is going downhill when you get a form-letter love note in the mail.

The old flames that haunt our memories most are usually the ones we didn't have a ghost of a chance with anyway.

Many a daughter's dreamboat has been drydocked by her dad.

Romance: just one fool thing after another.

Love is a lot like fishing: you're always thinking about the one that got away.

The most common cause of love at first sight is a poorly lit room.

When teens dance, they don't talk and they don't touch. It's like being married for thirty years.

If love is blind, marriage is like a trip to the optometrist.

Don't take it too seriously when a pretty girl smiles at you. She may just be getting ready to laugh out loud.

What Big Ben said to the Leaning Tower of Pisa: "I've got the time if you've got the inclination."

Remember, a lot of guys who look like princes end up being toads.

Love is like toothpaste: a squeeze will usually get you a little more.

Wolf: someone who wants you to play ball without providing the diamond.

Love: that feeling that makes you care about someone else almost as much as you do about yourself.

Many a girl who has tired of trying to get a pearl out of an oyster has settled for getting a diamond out of an old crab.

Noah's Ark was probably the last cruise ship with enough males to go around.

For some people love is a precipice; for others it's a bluff.

In spring a young man's fancy lightly turns . . . and does it without even signaling first.

If all the world loves a lover, why is everyone always so angry on those TV soap operas?

Love is like a fine wine: first it goes to your head, and then it goes to your wallet.

Birds and the bees: he calls her honey, and she starts wanting to build a nest.

Love is a two-way street . . . that's why they put up all the yield signs.

Love is blind . . . that's why all the world loves a louver.

There may be other fish in the sea, but that's not too comforting if you're a worm.

Did you ever notice that the people who can light up your life always know where your switch is?

Platonic relationship: when you date only dead philosophers . . . or it seems like it.

Sure, there are lots of other fish in the sea, but lots of them are barracudas and sharks.

Love often goes from first blush to seeing red.

If love is blind, how come the cosmetics industry is so huge?

Then there was the X-ray technician who fell in love with a patient, but her friends couldn't figure what she saw in him.

Computer dating is all right, but from the look of some of these folks they could use carbon dating.

There are plenty of fish in the sea, but they aren't all waiting with baited breath.

If you're unlucky in love, remember there are plenty of other fish in the sea; but then, who wants to hug scales?

Love is like a door: first it's swinging, then there's a catch.

Love is like high school: it begins as sport, turns into chemistry, and ends up as home economics.

For some people, love is a match made in heaven; for others, it's a butane lighter from hell.

For some people, love is a feast; for others, it's like a bowl of cold oatmeal.

If you can hear bells ringing, either it's love or your hat's on too tight.

There are plenty of other fish in the sea, but it's going to cost you a lot of clams.

Love may be the language of the soul, but it's also the language of the heel.

The difference between a man walking and a man kissing: one misses the bus, the other busses the miss.

Have you ever noticed how the people who believe in love at first sight always have second sight?

A pretty girl is like a melody . . . and the melody is "Diamonds Are a Girl's Best Friend."

Many young ladies have a tale to tell about the wolf who cried, "Boy!"

Some supermarkets have actually become singles' scenes. Now there's a meat market at the meat market.

These days, love is many-spended thing.

If the way to a man's heart is through his stomach, then love makes the world grow round.

Young lovers' advice: the call of the wild often turns into the crawl of the child.

MARRIAGE, DIVORCE, AND BEYOND

Divorce: when your better half becomes your bitter half.

Alimony: when your former spouse is living beyond your means.

If we really want to cut down on the divorce rate, they should issue marriage licenses with expiration dates.

You can always tell the father of the bride at a wedding. He's the one who keeps looking in his wallet and crying.

A fifteenth wedding anniversary is tough to celebrate. It's too early to brag and too late to complain.

Marrying a girl for her looks is like buying a house for its paint.

A May-December marriage used to mean one between a young woman and an old man. Now it means one that lasts an entire eight months.

Alimony is like paying installments on a car after you've wrecked it.

Groom: someone who lost his liberty in the pursuit of happiness.

If you really want to combine marriage and career, become a professional bigamist.

Don't be too hard on your spouse. After all, what can you expect of someone who was raised by your mother-in-law?

A lot of women don't live up to their marriage vows. Both parties take an oath to grow old together and then she lets her husband go ahead without her.

Some couples lead very quiet lives . . . they don't speak to each other.

Marriage has turned many an old rake into a lawn mower.

Alimony: bounty on the mutiny.

A wedding ceremony is where you promise to love, honor, and oh boy.

Everyone should get married at least once. They're already into reruns on "Divorce Court."

Marriage is dedicated to the proposition that all men are berated equal.

A successful marriage is based on the ability to pretend you don't know what your spouse is thinking.

You know the honeymoon's over when he trades the belle of the ball for the bowl of the ball.

Every man should get married . . . then he wouldn't have to blame everything on the government.

People who marry for better or worse usually can't do any worse and couldn't do any better.

Maybe there'd be fewer divorces if marriage counselors would only quit urging spouses to talk to each other.

Marriage is a dialogue. Divorce is two monologues.

There's nothing wrong with being a model spouse . . . as long as you don't come unglued.

Fifty percent of all marriages end in divorce, but one hundred percent of all divorces begin with marriage.

Love makes the heart race . . . and marriage makes the heart give up racing.

Wedding expenses: the bill of rites.

People who wake up and smell the coffee are lucky to have someone else making it for them.

Marriages may be made in heaven, but prenuptial agreements are drawn up in the other place . . . lawyers' offices.

Adultery is like an adult tree . . . they both involve grown-up saps.

Everybody talks about the game of love, but nobody talks about the consolation prize of marriage.

Isn't it strange that just about the time the magic goes out of a marriage, the tricks begin?

Two can live as cheaply as one . . . as long as one of them stops eating.

Opposites attract . . . but what they attract are divorce lawyers.

Fed ex: a former spouse who works for the government.

Marriage is when you play the game of love; divorce is when you get the referee.

A spouse who promises to stop drinking is a lot like spaghetti: they string you along before hitting the sauce.

The counselor told the couple their marriage would have a better chance of succeeding if they had similar interests, so they both took up philandering.

Tools of a marriage: the bonds of matrimony, and the file for divorce.

The world would be a happier place if there was a mandatory waiting period before obtaining a gun or a marriage license.

Show me a married man and I'll show you someone who squeaks for himself.

If you really want to become a philosopher, get married.

If you really want to lead a stable life, marry a horse.

Open marriage: one where you let your spouse talk occasionally.

The wedding is when you pick your pattern of dishes; the marriage is when you pick on your spouse's patterns of behavior.

They call marriage an institution because that's where you feel you've been committed to.

The person who stands next to the groom at a Quaker wedding: Friend's best man.

Thirty-five percent of all marriages end in divorce. The other sixty-five percent fight it out to the bitter end.

The reason there are so many June weddings is that it's hard to think in the heat.

Just remember, "marriage" and "mirage" have a lot of the same letters.

An old-fashioned marriage is one in which he insists on being the breadwinner, and expects her to make the sandwiches.

Marriage: that's when somebody lights up your life and then starts sending you electric bills.

If you don't believe there's a theory of relativity, just try marrying someone from a large family.

If you think the magic has gone out of your marriage, you can always pull a disappearing act.

Some folks think marriage gives you a new leash on life.

Then there was the bigamist stand-up comic who said, "Take my wives . . . please!"

Too many marriages are on the rocks because too many people are having too many on the rocks.

Wedding: where a father gives away his daughter . . . along with a sizable portion of his accumulated wealth.

Lifelong bachelor: someone who held out for the perfect person.

Lots of people who marry live happily ever after . . . usually after the divorce.

Love is a state of mind, and marriage is when you feel like moving to another state.

'Tis better to have loved and lost . . . unless you're paying the alimony.

Bachelor party: where a bunch of guys get together and demonstrate all the reasons not to get married.

Alimony: divorce on the installment plan.

Love is when you know you were made for each other. Marriage is when you start making the alterations.

The closest to perfection you ever get is right before the wedding.

Kids complain about parents' making all their decisions for them, and then grow up and marry someone who does the same thing.

Marriage means standing by your partner through thick and thin . . . thickening middles and thinning hair.

What's so bad about spouses' talking in their sleep? It may be the only time they say something interesting.

Marriages may be made in heaven, but the only repair shops are here on earth.

Romance may burn like fire, but eventually someone has to pay the heating bill.

Marriage is like a cafeteria. You pick out something that looks good, and pay for it down the line.

Most married couples can read each other like a book . . . that's why they watch so much TV.

The difference between engagement and marriage is like the difference between puppy love and being housebroken.

A good marriage requires communication, but most spouses' transmitters are better than their receivers.

There are plenty of fish in the sea, but most of them want you to make a down payment on a nice little aquarium for two.

Cross word puzzle: when arguing couples try to figure out what nasty thing to say next.

Statistics show that couples who sleep on waterbeds tend to drift apart.

Most guys who get a trophy wife end up with consolation-prize kids.

Open marriage: that's when every time you open your mouth, your spouse doesn't close it for you.

You know you're headed for divorce when you ask for separate checks from the marriage counselor.

If love is a two-way street, then marriage counselors are highway maintenance.

Some people marry their better halves; others just marry for better quarters.

Marriage is on the increase; buy stock in toaster ovens.

If you don't think you can put a price on love, then you've never paid alimony.

The honeymoon's over when you realize that all the tough times you see each other through wouldn't even occur if you were still single.

Marriage is the surest way to learn that love is blind.

Trade relations: what you do when you get remarried.

People in love aim to please. Married people aim to wound.

Marriage counselors tell couples to spend more time together, but it's the time spent together that made the counseling necessary in the first place.

After you've been married a few years, you can understand every word your spouse isn't saying.

Marriage is like a midnight phone call: you get a ring and then you wake up.

There's nothing wrong with the institution of marriage that a change in personnel won't fix.

Things could have been worse for Adam. He didn't have a mother-in-law and Eve couldn't tell him how lousy he was compared to her first husband.

Spouse: a former lover.

The first domestic dispute was when Eve kept putting Adam's pants in the salad by mistake.

Marriage is like the army: everyone complains, but you'd be surprised how many reenlist.

The penalty for bigamy is two mothers-in-law.

Husbands who go shopping with their wives are in for a browse-beating.

KEEP IT IN THE FAMILY

Dinnertime: when kids join their parents at the table to watch them eat.

The only thing more depressing than a home without children is a home with them.

The only time children can be seen and not heard is when they're asleep.

Ask not for whom the bell tolls. If there's a teenager in the house, it's a phone call for them.

If kids really want to learn to swear, they should get a job either on the docks or at the golf course.

Out of the mouths of babes come things they shouldn't have heard us say in the first place.

Wouldn't it be great if all children behaved like you think you did when you were a kid?

If you want to teach your kids to count, give them different allowances.

Families with babies and families without babies are always feeling sorry for each other.

Kids need to eat their vegetables so they'll grow up strong enough to make their kids eat their vegetables.

You know your kids are growing up when your daughter starts putting on lipstick and your son starts wiping it off.

Social Security: a kid with the only football on the block.

School days can be the best days of your life, provided your kids are old enough to go.

Sound travels very slowly. The things you tell your kids when they're teenagers seem to reach them about the time they're forty.

The FBI has over 100 million fingerprints. So does every home with two or more kids.

Adolescence: when a boy refuses to believe that someday he'll be as dumb as his father.

The teens are an awkward age. Kids know how to make phone calls but not how to end them.

No wonder most teenagers think their parents are birdbrained; the parents are watching them like hawks.

Report card: a piece of paper that lets you realize you don't have to be a weight lifter to raise a dumbbell.

You know your daughter has reached adolescence when she's all skin and phones.

Early to bed and early to rise . . . probably means there's a baby in the house.

You know your kids are entering adolescence when they think you're entering obsolescence.

The hardest part about having kids isn't the delivery . . . it's that you have to keep paying postage.

The most amazing thing about a baby is that they're constantly changing . . . and you're constantly changing them.

Kids who play in puddles prove that into every rain some life must fall.

Most kids think all salads should be tossed.

These days, a model child is one without a police record.

Kids and condiments: jam session.

There is already an alien life-form on this planet . . . it's called a teenager.

Bottled emotions: when babies cry for their milk.

Wealthy families claim having kids is a heir-raising experience.

Transparent: when your kids can see right through you.

Free speech: what teenagers get from their parents when they come home late.

Our children have it easy. When we were kids, we had to be driven to school because our parents were too poor to buy us our own cars.

Are your kids listening to too much hard rock? It's a simple case of metal illness.

If vacations were really about getting away from it all, families would split up and take separate trips.

The difference between being the parent of a toddler and the parent of a teenager: one is a caregiver, the other is a car giver.

Change is a good thing . . . particularly when it comes to baby's diapers.

The only thing kids throw and then pick up again: tantrums.

Drooling babies are the spitting image of their parents.

For some parents, child guidance consists of showing them how to use the TV remote.

Teenage definition of adult: a dolt.

Kids don't hate vegetables, they just hate to eat them.

And if you're a cow, you think children should be seen and not herded.

Lots of parents want their kids to follow in their footsteps . . . but it takes time to learn to sidestep.

The perfect gift for parents who spend quality time with their children: a quality timer.

Many parents are trying to get classical-music appreciation in their children's curriculum . . . a sort of Bach-to-school movement.

You've got to make allowances for kids . . . and as far as they're concerned, the bigger the better.

About the only place you really get on-the-job training anymore is parenting.

Curse of the mummy: when female parents swear.

If you get out of the room when a baby throws a tantrum, it's known as leaving the scene of the cryin'.

I don't know what to think of this younger generation. I guess we'll have to wait until they're old enough to talk.

Teenagers work their fingers to the phone.

Times have changed. Kids used to play house . . . now they play real estate developer.

There must be something to evolution; otherwise, why would so many parents go ape over their kids' behavior?

Have you heard about the new sleep-deprivation experiment? It's called parenting.

Adolescence is an embarrassing time of life. That's when everyone's parents turn stupid simultaneously.

Truth hurts. Ask any kid who's ever been spanked.

These days the only way to get the red-carpet treatment is to give your kids cherry Popsicles.

If you really want to make sure your kids don't read dirty books, make them required reading on the school curriculum.

It's getting so expensive to have children that many people prefer to lease them on a part-time basis.

Some fathers parent with an iron fist . . . like a nine-iron on the golf course while Mom's home with the kids.

Some babies are brought by the stork. They're the ones who grow up to be for the birds.

People with kids know Mother is the necessity of intervention.

Kidnapping is a serious offense . . . particularly if the kid's caught napping during class.

Most kids operate on a need-to-now basis.

In these times the accent may be on youth, but the stress is on parents.

The best way to make kids understand the value of money is to charge stuff to their credit cards.

The best way to get your teenager to shovel the driveway is to tell him he can use the car.

If you want to start your kids in the right direction, lie about your past.

Brat: someone else's kid. Your brat: a sensitive, high-strung little darling.

Of course there's a sucker born every minute. How else are you supposed to get the milk out of the bottle?

There's nothing wrong with talking to yourself. Lots of people do it; they're called parents.

You know your kids are growing up when you stop telling them nighttime stories and they start telling you stories of where they've been that night.

Life has its ups and downs . . . particularly for new parents in the middle of the night.

If cleanliness is next to godliness, we'd better start praying for our children.

Curbing your impulses: when teenagers go parking.

Babies who like to climb are innocents in ascents, in a sense.

Mother: someone who bears children . . . up until they move away from home.

Most kids learn their lessons at their father's knee . . . either sitting or getting spanked.

Kids have it easy; their lives are held together by mitten clips.

Parents should learn to laugh at themselves a little. After all, their kids do.

When you get married you trade the call of the wild for the crawl of the child.

If you can see the writing on the wall . . . you have kids with crayons.

It used to be you told your kids about the birds and bees . . . now it's the vultures and the vermin.

All kids have a PG rating . . . parental guidance suggested.

Some mothers think the most important thing they can instill in their daughters is the will to shop.

When kids go through potty training: the Toilet Zone.

It used to be that growing up meant getting all your questions answered. Now it means getting all your answers questioned.

What would a home be without children . . . besides quiet, I mean?

Mallpractice: when kids play shopping center.

One good thing about having kids: you've got live-in food and entertainment critics.

By the time a kid can tell time, there's nothing to say to it anymore.

You have to be understanding of boys when they're going through that awkward age . . . fifteen to forty-five.

The best time to try to change someone is when they're a baby . . . and then frequently.

We want our kids to have all the things we didn't have as children . . . like good grades.

The younger generation has gotten so lazy they only have sit-down comics.

Trickle-down theory: when toddlers potty-train.

Horn of plenty: what you hear when your teenaged daughter's date arrives to pick her up.

Children already have too many advantages. For instance, they don't have to raise children.

Psychiatrists tell us there are no bad children . . . only little monsters cleverly disguised to genetically resemble us.

You've got to make allowances for kids . . . payable weekly.

By the time a baby is born, most mothers have had a bellyful.

There's nothing wrong with the younger generation that can't be improved by the older generation's shutting up occasionally.

Teenager: a kid who looks at her parents and hopes genetics isn't true.

The best way to avoid car sickness is to not let your kids drive it.

First-time parents: ones who are anxious for their kid to talk.

Kids always know when there's company in the house. They can hear their parents actually talking to each other.

If you really want to know how a man reacts under pressure, watch him while he helps with his kid's science project.

Teenager: one who is well informed about anything he doesn't have to study.

What's the big argument over environment versus heredity? Parents provide both anyway.

For a teenager, the key to popularity is the one that fits the ignition.

Garage sale: where money changes hands, and objects are moved from one garage to another.

People find that living in glass houses is a real pane.

Major renovation: a simple home repair you've tried to do yourself.

Hick town: where there's no good place to do bad.

If it ain't broke, just let your husband tinker with it and it soon will be.

Hometown: where people wonder how you made it as far as you did.

Our great strides in transportation have one sure drawback: there's no such thing as a distant relative anymore.

Small town: where it's no sooner done than said.

There are three ways to get something done: do it yourself, hire someone, or forbid your kids to do it.

Variety may be the spice of life, but monotony buys the groceries.

It's too bad the hand-cranked ice-cream maker is obsolete. It was a great way to teach kids that work has its rewards.

Alarm clock: a device designed to wake up people who don't have children.

Family man: one who replaces the money in his wallet with snapshots.

Garage sale: pick of the litter.

Some people come from stable families and some people come from families without horses.

Once we were told to go forth and multiply. Now it's go forth and subdivide.

If family members really expressed how they felt, more in-laws would be outlaws.

Opportunity knocks only once . . . after that, it's your neighbor wanting to borrow the lawn mower.

The first person to discover fire isn't such a big deal. How about the first guy who dropped his dinner in the fire and invented the barbecue?

Some people come home to unwind; others come home to unravel.

Love thy neighbor, or else you'll never get back the power tools you loaned him.

Some people trace their family trees, and others can afford only to look up their family shrub.

Daddy's birthday gift: the tie that blinds.

Home is that warm feeling you get when you walk in the door and everyone ignores you.

If you want to live in a better neighborhood but can't afford it, buy a camper.

Lots of families go in for water sports . . . like dishwashing and baby bathing.

One thing's for sure: this generation won't have any trouble cooking just the way Mom used to . . . as long as they can read the microwave instructions.

What people learn when they remodel their house: they'd like to remodel their spouse.

Shake any family tree and you're bound to get a few nuts.

The great thing about microwaves is now you can be a lousy cook in much less time.

People who live in gas houses shouldn't throw matches.

One thing about do-it-yourself home improvements: you begin to realize there are no right angles . . . only wrong ones.

Maybe the grass is always greener on the other side of the fence because your neighbor never returns the gardening tools he borrowed.

Blood is thicker than water, but every family has its drips.

Lots of people come from broken homes. Who has the time to do the repairs?

What's the big deal about pumping iron? House spouses do it every time they press a shirt.

If a man's home is his castle, why is he also the joker who has to pay the mortgage?

If you build a better mousetrap, your relatives will beat a path to your door.

Family ties are hard to break, but you can always cut them up and throw them away.

When fathers tell jokes: popcorn.

They have a new cheap-housing development in the Sudan: "Low Rents of Arabia."

Even if your parents do tell you about the birds and bees, they never mention the mortgages on those hives and aviaries.

It takes a heap of living to make a house a home . . . it also takes a heap of mortgage payments.

It's a jungle out there . . . particularly if your lawn mower's broken.

Did you hear about the old tycoon who wanted more grandchildren? He was worried about his receding heir line.

Statistics show that two out of three families live next door.

Success is relative . . . the more success, the more relatives.

Iron will: one the relatives can't break.

People who live in grass houses shouldn't throw power lawn mowers.

The problem with family trees is some relative is always trying to prune off the deadwood.

Show me a backyard barbecue and I'll show you a family who has gone to the dogs . . . and the burgers.

Our forefathers cut down the wilderness so we could plant saplings in our housing developments.

If you want the world to beat a path to your door, build your house on a jogging trail.

Realtor: someone who's always putting someone in their place.

Distant relative: one who has more money than you do.

If insanity isn't hereditary, how come your relatives can drive you crazy?

We will all return to the dust . . . unless you have someone who cleans for you.

Then there was the man who wanted to drown his sorrows, but he couldn't get his in-laws to get into the sack.

Homesickness: what you feel about ten minutes after you've signed the loan papers for the new house.

Family values: when restaurants give kiddie discounts.

Family planning: figuring out how to keep the kids occupied for the entire weekend.

It's the law: build an extra bedroom, go to mother-in-law jail.

Kids sure have it easy these days. When we were their age, we had to walk miles back and forth to the TV set because there were no remote channel changers.

Money down the drain: whenever you call the plumber.

United we stand, divided we fall . . . and subdivided we're a real estate development.

Family reunion: nest of kin.

There are lots of women who combine family and a career. They're called mothers.

Refrigerator: a place to store leftovers until you throw them out.

Small town: where everyone knows whose credit is good and whose children aren't.

In these modern times it may not be as important who wears the pants in the family, but people are still touchy about who wears the dresses.

The only good thing about being henpecked is that you get plenty of eggs.

Lots of people build their dream house and then get insomnia trying to figure out how to pay for it.

Seventy-eight percent of the earth is covered with water, and the other twenty-two percent is covered with mortgages.

Man is always trying to improve his lot . . . that's why they invented gardening shops.

Microwave-meal server: someone who can dish it out but who can't cook it.

IN SICKNESS AND IN HEALTH

Time may heal all wounds, but it takes a plastic surgeon to remove the scar tissue.

Most plastic surgeons get you to pay through the nose.

Dentists take great pains in their work.

Psychiatrist: somebody who asks you a lot of expensive questions that your spouse asks you for free.

Hypochondriac: someone who takes different pills than you do.

With the price of apples these days, you might as well just call the doctor.

No matter how much a hospital charges for a private room, they still only give you a semiprivate gown.

People who go to acupuncturists are always holier-than-thou.

If more people kept their nose to the grindstone, plastic surgeons would lose a lot of business.

Doctors call it a *check*up because that's what you give up one of every time you go.

In olden times, doctors used to bleed people for every minor affliction . . . and they still do.

It is the physician's cause to heal, but it's the physician's cost that makes him well-heeled.

Dental surgery: tough day at the orifice.

Obstetrician: a doctor making money in the stork market.

When dentists retire, they are given a twenty-one-gum salute.

Doctors' conference on infection: staph meeting.

Egyptian bone doctor: Cairo practor.

Next time your doctor says you're healthy as a horse, try paying him in oats.

Then there's the plastic surgeon nicknamed "skycap" because he's removed so many bags.

You can call a doctor a quack, but you still can't duck his bill.

The problem with chiropractors is they're always doing things behind your back.

Plastic surgeons are experts at saving face.

There was a dentist who moonlighted as a cocktail pianist. The problem was, with either job he was always tickling the ivories.

Gastrointestinal medicine is a good career if you've got the stomach for it.

Doctor who specializes in phobias: afraidian psychologist.

If truth is beauty, why are there so many rich plastic surgeons?

If laughter really were the best medicine, doctors would figure out a way to charge for it.

If hospitals are places to get well, why do they serve that food?

We don't want to say that hospitals have become like factories, but they now itemize their bills into parts and labor.

If you're really healthy as a horse, why aren't you going to a vet?

Plastic surgeon: cosmedic.

Having children is a very enriching experience . . . enriching to the doctor and hospital, that is.

Did you hear about the two podiatrists who were arch rivals?

Who says the appendix is useless? Look at all the doctors' condos it's paid for.

You know you're in trouble when they make you pay your hospital bill before you're admitted.

Podiatrists are good at thinking on your feet.

When your doctor tells you you're as healthy as a horse, it's time to stop eating so much oat bran.

Sign in podiatrist's office: "Caution: Toe Zone."

Doctor's waiting room: where patients test their patience.

Sign on dentist's office: "Drill Team."

Nature gave us a biological clock; doctors give painkillers to turn off the alarm.

Podiatrists have got a real foothold in the medical profession.

Pain threshold: doorway to dentist's office.

Plastic surgeon: one who accepts credit cards.

The medical profession sure is getting specialized. Now there's an ear and throat doctor who caters to gossips.

Surgeons have to make incision decisions.

Let's hope our doctors' medical techniques are more up-to-date than the magazines in their waiting rooms.

Dentist: someone who puts your money where your mouth is.

The difference between dentists and other people is that when they're feeling down in the mouth, it's yours.

The first thing you learn about being in a hospital is that the gowns didn't exactly come from Paris.

Nowadays, when you get some color in your cheeks, you have to run to the doctor to make sure it's not high blood pressure.

They call them wisdom teeth because taking them out helps pay for the dentist's kids' education.

If time really did heal all wounds, doctors wouldn't keep you in the waiting room so long.

Dentists go to great pains in their work.

Hypochondriac: someone who's sending his doctor's kids through school.

Anesthetists' motto: "Numb's the word."

If you're scared of the orthodontist, you've got a mental block about the dental doc.

Thanks to the miraculous strides in medicine, people live longer . . . giving them the extra time needed to pay their medical bills.

In these confused times, the only people you can see eye to eye with are optometrists.

Just about the time you finally wake up and smell the coffee, your doctor orders you off caffeine.

An apple a day may keep the doctor away, but dip that thing in taffy and you'll sure make a dentist your friend.

When eye doctors have affairs: optome-tryst.

Retired army animal doctor: vet vet.

Doctors' work involves long hours . . . mainly for the patients in the waiting room.

Doctors say we should walk for our health. After paying the doctor bill, who can afford to drive?

Psychiatrists usually begin therapy with your childhood because they're getting paid by the hour.

Did you hear about the hospital dance where everyone showed up wearing the same gown?

Organ transplant: insider trading.

Plastic surgeon: someone who wants you to stick your nose in their business.

Hospitals ought to put their recovery rooms right next to the cashier's office.

Never argue with your doctor . . . he has inside information.

Socialized medicine: when people sit around at a bridge party and talk about their operations.

Pain is just nature's way of telling you not to move any more than absolutely necessary.

The common cold: nose pollution.

OF SOUND MIND AND BODY

Pessimist: someone who looks at life through woes-colored glasses.

Give a pessimist an inch . . . and he'll measure it.

Conscience doesn't keep you from doing anything wrong, it just keeps you from enjoying it.

There's a big difference between "I've just seen my way clear" and "My mind's gone blank."

Vegetarian: someone who has a beef with beef.

Overweight: when everything you eat goes to waist.

"A penny for your thoughts": Something you'll never hear a psychiatrist say.

Chew the fat: what you do at a greasy spoon.

The least-healthful position to sleep in is with your feet on the office desk.

Why are women's magazines fifty pages of recipes and fifty pages of diets?

It's bad luck to be superstitious.

If you greet everyone with a smile, you're either a happy person or you just got your teeth capped.

People who get up early in the morning invariably crow about it.

You're overweight when you're living beyond your seams.

Pessimist: someone who builds dungeons in the air.

Nostalgia: when you find the present tense and the past perfect.

Dieting: waiting for your hips to come in.

It's not so terrible to be stubborn. At least you know what you'll be thinking tomorrow.

At least an egotist doesn't go around talking about other people.

It's all right for your mind to go blank, as long as you turn off the sound.

Did you ever notice the people who drive to health clubs and search frantically for the closest parking space to the door?

You know you're getting overweight when you roll with the paunches.

A lot of people who have open minds should have them closed for remodeling.

Depression: when you have to face the music, and it's a polka.

Humor: the ability to laugh at other people.

The mind is like a television . . . lots of reruns and static.

At least a schizophrenic knows how the other half lives.

Why is it that people who drink to forget never forget to drink?

What's so great about feeling fit as a fiddle? Who wants to be high-strung and whiny?

If you exercise, you'll add ten years to your life . . . but you'll spend those ten years exercising.

A sure cure for feeling listless: write a list.

Lots of people keep their figure . . . it's just that some keep it buried deeper than others.

Given the popularity of fad diets, you'd think the sleek were going to inherit the earth.

Some people think a well-rounded life need not include exercise. And you have to admit, they are well-rounded.

Video aerobics: getting up and down out of your recliner chair to change tapes.

If you want food that melts in your mouth, eat it right out of the freezer.

There's a new fad in Los Angeles: on days with no smog, the citizens indulge in binge breathing.

Some people are good at keeping their figure . . . and some are better at multiplying it.

It's hard to know who's wasting their breath more . . . smokers, or the people trying to get them to quit.

Aerobics class: re-form school.

Hangover: that part of the stomach that no longer fits under the belt.

Overeater's motto: "Waste not, want not."

Some things you just know deep down inside . . . like when you're hungry.

You know it's time to go on a diet when the neighborhood kids are playing circus and they want to use your coat as a tent.

Contradiction of terms: drinking to your health.

All those things that melt in your mouth have a way of solidifying once they're inside.

Diet book: a word to the wides.

There's a new exercise course for comedians . . . you learn how to keep in trim by being a cutup.

Neurotic: when that little voice in your head keeps laughing at you.

If the right half of the brain controls the left side of the body, and the left half of the brain controls the right side of the body, does that mean that left-handed people are the only ones in their right mind?

Spiral staircases are for people who want to be getting somewhere while still going around in circles.

Shrink wrap: psychiatrist's overcoat.

Nowadays, lots of people are beside themselves trying to find themselves.

Neurotic: when you call a plumber to fix your pipe dreams.

Depression: when you've finally made it to the mountaintop and you discover it's an active volcano.

There's one good thing about masochism: you always hurt the one you love.

Even-tempered: when you always look grumpy.

Some people have one-track minds . . . with nothing but empty boxcars.

Some people are so selfish they don't care about anyone else . . . but that's *their* problem.

You know you're losing it when you start talking to yourself and even you aren't listening.

How come people who want to drown their sorrows always look for someone to go swimming with them?

Psychiatry may not cure schizophrenia, but at least it lets you know how the other half lives.

Psychiatrists have discovered that only one out of four people have inferiority complexes. The rest really are inferior.

If there's a light at the end of the tunnel, you can be sure someone's going to send you the electric bill for it.

"Why did the chicken cross the road?" . . . an eggs-istential question.

Psychiatry school: where they learn the nuts and bolts of nuts.

Some people have split personalities . . . when it's time to help out, they split.

Optimist: someone who can always put a happy face on other people's bad luck.

The average diet consists of the four basic food groups: fat, oil, grease, and cholesterol.

To prehistoric man, health clubs were big sticks of wood to beat predators off with.

Vegetarians: the beet generation.

Things used to be simpler when you just went down to the gym and lifted some barbells. Now you have to go to the fitness center and aerobically tone muscle groups.

School phys-ed clothes: class action suit.

The only exercise some people get is exercising caution.

He eats like a horse. He'd eat like a cow, but he doesn't have the stomach for it.

People who constantly go on and off diets live life in the fat lane.

Did you hear about the restaurant where all the waiters know the Heimlich maneuver? It's got a no-choking section.

Lunch for gossips: tongue sandwich.

Most people are serious about getting into shape . . . into the shape of a potato.

If you wear dentures, a glass of water is something you can really sink your teeth into.

The reason you exercise is to exorcise the extra size.

The best way to get rid of those unwanted pounds is to exercise them off . . . thus the expression "sore loser."

We've grown tired of all this talk about nutrition. Let's get some of that old trition back.

Cook's motto: "To herb is cumin."

Doctors say we should watch what we eat, but how many people eat with their eyes closed, anyway?

Carnivorous: when you eat in your car, as from a drive-through restaurant.

The only people living off the fat of the land anymore are dietitians.

Most people have no trouble lowering their cholesterol . . . into their mouths.

Some people go on diets right away and others are just biting their time.

New dieters' motto: "Waist not, taste not."

Lots of people talk about the food chain, but how often do you see them eating one?

Some books give you food for thought, except cookbooks, which give you thought for food.

If you really want to make an impression, gain three hundred pounds.

An apple a day will keep the doctor away . . . assuming, of course, that it hasn't been grown in chemical soil, sprayed with pesticides, and then covered with wax.

What all diets promise: the shape of things to come.

Why is it as soon as you move past your salad days you move right into your potato days?

If we really need more fiber in our diet, I'll eat my hat.

Lots of women have hourglass figures . . . it's just that, for some, the hour is up.

The difference between a dieter and a sentry: one watches his weight, the other waits his watch.

What about the cannibal kid who wasn't allowed to join in games with the missionary's son because his mother didn't want him playing with his food.

Aerobic workouts aren't a new invention. Back on the farm, they call them chores.

Did you hear about the restaurant that didn't serve pork? They had a hams-off policy.

A stitch in time saves you from jogging any further, if the stitch is in your side.

It can be disheartening trying to diet, but you just have to keep your chins up.

What's the big deal about liquid diets? Lots of people go on liquid diets. They're called drunks.

Doctors say too much caffeine is bad for you, meaning it's time to put the coffee brakes on those coffee breaks.

With most of these fancy gyms, the only thing guaranteed to get slimmer is your wallet.

Did you hear about the guy whose doctor told him to go on a liquid diet, so he melted all his ice cream?

Figure of speech: when you only talk about dieting.

Depression: going to an all-you-can-eat buffet at the Sprout Cafe.

For some people, their diets are all behind them now.

Chewing the fat: what you do before wearing it.

Some people like to eat low-fat diets and some are members of the frequent-fryer program.

Fast-food franchises live off the fat of the land.

If you really want to be with the movers and the shakers, join an aerobics class.

Cold soft-boiled eggs are beyond repoach.

Saturday-night date: what you eat before Sunday-morning prunes.

Many men, when they get thin on top, compensate by getting thick on the bottom.

Fatness: the past tense of fitness.

What's so awful about being a paranoid? Two noids are better than one.

Most of us can't afford to be driven crazy, so we have to drive ourselves.

To some people, the only time for reflection is when they look into the bathroom mirror.

Sign on a psychiatrist's office: "Grow up and quit complaining!"

Some folks have a lot on their mind . . . a vacant lot.

Did you ever notice the similarity between compulsive behavior and repulsive behavior?

Loneliness: that feeling you have right before somebody barges in and reminds you how peaceful it was.

You know you're in trouble when you call a self-esteem hotline and get put on hold.

There's nothing wrong with your life being an open book . . . as long as you hang out with people who can't read.

Nostalgia: the ability to recall the past fondly, despite the facts.

Lots of people have open minds. The problem is, the opening is their mouth.

People who like to reminisce live life in the past lane.

Cry, and you cry alone; laugh, and your family wants to get you into psychiatric counseling.

Sign on a psychiatrist's office: "You're only young once, but you can be Jungian forever."

Pessimist's den: room for doubt.

Why have an identity crisis? That's why we carry driver's licenses.

If you're really fit to be tied, you're probably a shoe.

Did you hear about the volunteer at the dream clinic? He got hired for sleeping on the job.

It's all right to build castles in the air, but just try to get a construction loan on one.

Some people say those pop-psychology movements are for the birds, but they're really for the squirrels . . . because they gather all the nuts.

Cuckoo clock: timepiece in a psychiatrist's office.

What good is a button-down mind if you can't keep your lip zipped?

You shouldn't let people drive you crazy when you know it's only walking distance.

These self-help seminars do a world of good . . . for the bank accounts of the folks who run them.

Neurosis: when you realize that life is a great journey, and you're sure you've lost your boarding pass.

If you look at the world too often through rose-colored glasses, you'll end up seeing red.

Psychiatrists' motto: "You're only Jung once, but that's nothing to be a Freud of."

People who make a living trying to get you to unwind are probably just stringing you along.

Learn to laugh at yourself . . . before somebody else beats you to it.

There's nothing wrong with having a second childhood. After all, it's a lot more attractive than a second infancy.

Everybody needs someone they can tell their troubles to. That's why mirrors were invented.

It used to be you could read someone like a book. Now you just watch them like a video.

People who live in glass houses know it's curtains for them.

You know it's going to be a bad day when you wake up looking like the photos on the post office wall.

Some people have such open minds they should be closed for remodeling.

They've now invented solo wrestling for people who need to get a grip on themselves.

Then there was the multiple-personality case who just wanted to be loved for himself.

Freudian slip: what you buy at a psychoanalytical lingerie shop.

Change is a good thing . . . particularly if you're planning on taking the bus.

If you're living in a dream world, you're a neurotic. If you're making a living in a dream world, you're a psychiatrist.

Why can't people solve their own problems? People who go to psychiatrists ought to have their heads examined.

People change, which is just as well . . . otherwise their clothes would smell pretty unpleasant.

People who build castles in the air usually can't afford the real estate underneath.

Depression is having a mental block and finding out it's your head.

Patience is a virtue that takes too long to learn.

An optimist is a father who lets his son take the new car on a date. A pessimist is one who won't. A cynic is one who did.

You know it's time to go on a diet when your wife tells you to pull in your stomach and you already have.

You know you're overweight when they give you a group rate at the health club.

He diets religiously . . . he never eats in church.

Usually when someone has a screw loose, it's the one that holds the tongue.

Broad-mindedness: high-mindedness flattened by experience.

Diet: a short period of starvation, followed by a rapid gain of five pounds.

Girdle: accessory after the fat.

Some diets are so good they take your breadth away.

Cottage cheese diet: when you eat your curds and weigh.

Tantrum: pique performance.

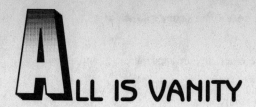

ALL IS VANITY

Some men hold their heads high so you can't see the bald spot.

Hindsight: why they put all those three-way mirrors in department stores.

The older a man gets, the more glorious his high-school football days become.

There's a big difference between looking cool and not looking so hot.

The best way to keep people from reading between the lines is to wear a lot of makeup.

The makers of hair-coloring products want us to believe that love is blond.

Beauty parlor: where you go when you have beauty pallor.

Everybody needs to get back to their roots . . . especially if they color their hair.

They have a new hairstyle for men with thinning hair . . . fluff and fold.

Lip service: cosmetics counter.

Plastic surgery: face-saving device.

Style is the ability to always look good. Fashion is the willingness to always look foolish.

Plastic surgery can take years off your appearance . . . and years off your life when you see the bill.

Oil slick: a dude with a pompadour.

Most people get plastic surgery in order to receive a more favorable interest rate.

Microwave: a tight hair permanent.

A cheap way to get a face-lift: stand on your head.

Tonsorial implant: hair apparent.

If there were such a thing as the fashion police, think how crowded it would be at the glamour slammer.

There's something new in plastic surgery: permanent-press faces.

Maybe there is no fountain of youth, but a couple of drinks will make most people less mature.

People who fish for compliments should learn how to scale them down.

Fashion show: an outfit night for mannered beast.

Some people dress to kill. The way others dress, it looks like they're trying to injure.

A compliment is like mouthwash: it feels great but sometimes it's tough to swallow.

One thing that separates us from the lower animals is our ability to wear such ridiculous clothes without laughing out loud.

Most people want to find their place in the sun just to show off their new bathing suit.

They say people who constantly gaze into mirrors are vain . . . but for most folks, you'd think that would be a cure for vanity.

Haberdashers make things that go to our heads.

All things come to those who wait . . . wrinkles, for instance.

The best way to look young is to hang around with old people.

Distinguished-looking: the last stage before extinguished-looking.

Why do people worry about having bags under their eyes? Pity the poor elephant . . . he has an entire trunk.

If time waits for no man, how come it stands still for a woman over thirty?

Lipstick: what happens when you kiss an ice cube.

Some of these new hairstyles look like they were cut in a blender.

Whoever said a woman's face is her fortune probably had to pay the cosmetics bills.

Fashion designers have come up with clothes so ugly this year that hanging's too good for them.

Country hair salon: where they dye with their boots on.

The fashion business isn't necessarily for the birds, but they've sure dressed a lot of turkeys.

YOU KNOW YOU'RE GETTING OLD WHEN . . .

The good old days: when you felt good and didn't look old.

When you're young you just want to set the world on fire. Then you get older and just want to live close to the fire department.

You know you're getting old when people don't accuse you of being lazy anymore because they just think you're tired.

You know you've reached middle age when, just as you're about to resist temptation, you fall asleep.

Class reunion: where everyone gets together to see who's falling apart.

You know you're getting old when they light your birthday candles and the automatic air-conditioning goes on.

If you really think old soldiers fade away, try getting into your old army uniform.

Middle age is when you'd do anything to feel better except give up what's making you feel lousy.

Nothing spoils a class reunion so much as the guy who both got rich and stayed youthful-looking.

An old-timer is someone who remembers when buying on time meant getting to the store before it closed.

You know you're getting old when you're at the bridge you were going to cross when you came to it.

You know you're getting old when, instead of telling you to slow down, the doctor tells you to speed up.

You know you're getting old when your idea of a night out is moving the TV out to the patio.

Patience is the ability to wait until you're too old to care anymore.

You know you're getting old when you talk about the good old days and nobody's qualified to call you a liar.

You know you've reached middle age when you're still trying to be a man on the move but you're constantly out of breath.

The main thing the older generation dislikes about the younger generation is their youth.

By the time the world is your oyster, you've lost the strength to crack open the shell.

You know you're getting old when you wake up feeling like a new man and he's more wrinkled than the first one.

Pessimist: a middle-aged optimist.

By the time you have money to burn, you're too old to play with matches.

Old-timer: someone who can remember every detail of his life story, but can't remember how many times he's told it to the same person.

By the time opportunity knocks, you'll probably have your hearing aid turned off.

You're only young once, but once is enough. After all, misspending your youth is how you got to look this way.

You know you're over the hill when people stop saying you're looking good and start saying you're looking well.

You know you're getting old when you say you feel healthy as a horse and your family sends you to the glue factory.

When you're young you can smell success close at hand. When you're older, you realize that smell is the sweat of all the guys ahead of you.

You know you're getting old when your mind tells you to stand on your own two feet and your body tells you to stay in the recliner chair.

Being over the hill is a lot better than being under it.

You know you're getting old when Boy Scouts try to help you cross the street.

You've reached middle age when all you exercise are your prerogatives.

If only we could grow smooth like coins as we wear out, we wouldn't mind life's rubs so much.

You know you're getting old when the years that used to turtle by now hurtle by.

Have you noticed that the now generation has grown into the now-and-then generation?

Salad days: back when you were fresh and had a lot of lettuce.

Middle age is that frustrating time when you're stuck between putting on the dog and giving up the ghost.

People nostalgic for the '60s are just longing for the good old daze.

You know you're getting old when you don't go out at night because your back did.

You know you're getting old when your entire future is behind you.

The worst part about being over the hill is you don't recall ever being on top of it.

Middle age: When you may not have any more skeletons in your closet, but your old clothes in there look like they were designed to fit them.

You know you're getting old when it takes longer to rest than it does to get tired.

By the time you're ready to relinquish your youth, your youth has already relinquished you.

If you're at the point where you're wondering if you've reached middle age, you're already past it.

You know you're getting old when you still have a lot of gas in the old tank but you need a new ignition system.

You know you're getting old when your little brother starts going bald.

Old age: when your memory is shorter and your stories are longer.

You know you're getting old when you no longer care what other people think of you, mainly because you've learned everyone's too busy thinking about themselves.

You know you're getting old when you start giving the advice you never followed as a youth.

You know you're getting old when the only time you get down is when you go to sleep.

You know you're getting old when "Here, here!" turns into "There, there!"

You know you're getting old when you can still "get down" but you can't get up again.

Most of us don't mind silver threads among the gold . . . it's when the carpet becomes threadbare.

You know you're getting old when time stops being on your side and starts getting on your tail.

You know you're getting old when memory lane stops at a dead end.

You know you're getting old when that come-hither look turns into a get-out-of-here glare.

By the time you're ready to stroll down memory lane, you have to crawl.

You know you're getting old when there's no question in your mind that there's no question in your mind.

Most folks don't mind the hands of time too much . . . it's the feet of crows.

By the time most of us have heard our calling we're already hard of hearing.

In spring a young man's fancy lightly turns, and a middle-aged man's fancy rolls over with a headache.

Nobody really minds the ticking of their biological clock . . . only when the alarm goes off.

Old age: when you finally know all the answers but you can't remember the questions.

The best way to stay young is to eat right, exercise, and lie about your age.

You know you're getting old when they start playing your favorite songs on the piped-in music at the supermarket.

You know you're getting old when you wake up looking like the picture on your driver's license.

Middle age: when you still have a lot on the ball, but you're too tired to roll it.

You know you're getting old when time flies whether you're having fun or not.

You know you're getting old when you go to your high school reunion and it looks like an archaeological dig.

Some people age well . . . and for others it's nip and tuck.

You know you're getting old when bingo is a way of life instead of a dog's name.

You know you're getting old when you finally hold all the cards . . . but they're get-well wishes.

By the time you can read your spouse like a book, you need bifocals.

Some people are retired when they just ought to be retreaded.

Why is it as soon as you move past your salad days you move right into your potato days?

Wrinkles are nature's way of focusing the picture. Plastic surgery is man's way of losing the prints.

Aging is about the only endeavor where you are guaranteed of advancement.

Memories are wonderful, if you can forget the right parts.

You're only young once, but if you keep that same wardrobe you can look foolish forever.

Flower power will rise again . . . about the time when the baby-boom generation is pushing up daisies.

As we get older, most of us don't mind the extra mileage on our bodies . . . it's the tread wear that bothers us.

Maybe no man is an island, but he still tends to get continental drift when middle age sets in.

It's not important where you stand . . . as long as you're still standing.

You know you're getting old when you go to a class reunion and they have a nurses' station next to the bar.

Just remember: even a black sheep turns gray.

You know you're getting old when, instead of avoiding temptation, it avoids you.

You know you've reached middle age when the only time you want to live life in the fast lane is at the grocery store.

They say there's no fool like an old fool, but you've got to remember that they've been practicing their whole lives.

You know you're getting old when you still chase girls, but only if it's downhill.

You know you're getting old when your fantasies consist of running away to a desert island . . . and catching up on sleep.

People keep looking for better ways of killing time, but time keeps winning the battle.

You know you're getting old when, instead of jumping to conclusions, you crawl to them.

You know you're getting old when your rock and roll turns to walk and stroll.

Retirement furniture: Rocker of Ages.

What you get with a ninety-year-old millionaire: a lot of gray heirs.

The worst part about retirement is that you find out how your spouse has been handling things at home all these years.

SPIRITUAL TRUTHS

If you believe Eve came from Adam's rib, then transplanting body parts is the oldest profession.

Time changes all things. For instance, when you're young adultery is a sin, but when you're old it's a miracle.

Don't be too hard on yourself; if people didn't sin, the churches would be out of business.

A little guy and a big guy decided to go into the fortune-telling business, so they advertised: "Small medium, and large."

Monastery: a home for unwed fathers.

Most people wouldn't long for immortality if they knew there was no TV in heaven.

Nothing makes it easier to resist temptation than a strong moral upbringing—and witnesses.

Lots of people bow their heads on Sunday, but they're usually putting on the golf course.

What to call a sister who has gone on to heaven: nun of the above.

You've got to say this for pants: at least they cover a multitude of shins.

At twenty, you want to be master of your fate and captain of your soul. At fifty, you'll settle for being master of your weight and captain of your bowling team.

Most people find it easier to pray for forgiveness than to fight temptation.

Lead us not into temptation . . . unless, of course, there's no possible way of getting caught.

They say cannibals used to eat a lot of missionaries. I guess one man's meat is another man's parson.

At least the wages of sin don't keep fluctuating with the economy.

Opportunist: someone who sold umbrellas before the Great Flood.

Some people are the down-to-earth type . . . and others prefer cremation.

Humility: the ability to fake shame over your accomplishments.

People are just like cars: when they meet their Maker, it's for a recall.

People who have to be led into temptation probably don't need to worry too much about it anyway.

Most people don't see the light without feeling a little heat first.

Intuition: that little voice telling you you're right, despite the truth.

Just about the time you learn the secret of life, it's over.

Lots of people can resist temptation . . . some even for as long as fifteen minutes.

Conscience: that small inner voice that you've been trying to get to shut up for years.

Faith: the ability to believe the ridiculous for the sublime.

Show me someone with a clear conscience and I'll show you someone with a lousy memory.

Truth is like elastic: you can stretch it a lot, but eventually it's going to come back on you.

Who says you can't take it with you? Have you checked out the price of caskets recently?

They say you can't take it with you. For a lot of us, even if we could it would melt.

There is a higher power . . . but with an unlisted phone number.

If you let your conscience be your guide, you're certainly going to be led through some uncharted territory.

The only problem with those guys who are always preaching harmony is that they always want to sing lead.

If they all shave their heads, why are they called Hairy Krishnas?

When the spirit moves you: drunks who dance.

If God had meant mankind to eat without working for it, He wouldn't have invented the artichoke.

God does answer our prayers . . . we just usually don't like the answer.

Conscience: the science of thinking up all the reasons not to have fun.

They say there's no rest for the wicked, but it's not exactly leisure world for the rest of us either.

Crapshooters' heaven: paradise with a pair of dice.

Let your conscience be your guide, unless you're a psychic, in which case you should let your unconscience be your guide.

Remember, you are not your brother's keeper . . . unless, of course, your brother lives in a zoo.

Psychic lecture: tele-vision.

It's not that most of us are afraid to die . . . we just don't want to die following a full day of nothing but errands.

Hell: spending eternity at your in-laws'.

Those who warn of the wages of sin obviously never worked in Las Vegas.

Most people aren't really afraid to meet their Maker . . . it's the other guy they don't want to run into.

We all have to give an accounting of our lives at the Pearly Gates. Unfortunately, they don't allow for deductions or shelters.

If there is anything to this reincarnation stuff, just hope your in-laws don't come back as mosquitoes.

Everything will return unto the dust . . . except sweaters, which will return unto the lint.

People who wrestle with their conscience usually go for two out of three falls.

Too many people lift their spirits by lifting their spirits.

Reincarnation may or may not be true, but some people should never have been carnated in the first place.

Newest craze to lift your spirits: exorcise videos.

Spare ribs: what man used to have before God created woman . . . and mother-in-law.

If you really want to see the light, take the shade off the lamp.

A loser is someone who tries spirit channeling and gets the public access channel.

Flood lights: how Noah illuminated his ark.

If God hadn't meant man to fly, He wouldn't have let us lay so many eggs.

Even if clouds did have silver linings, at the price of silver nowadays who could afford to mine them?

The last people who really turned over a new leaf were Adam and Eve.

They say it's always darkest before the dawn, but I say it's darkest when you haven't paid your electric bill.

They say we will all get our reward in heaven, but some of these TV evangelists aren't waiting that long.

Ministers take note: lousy sermons make for more bored-again Christians.

Some people use psychics to contact the spirit world . . . and others just use bartenders.

The average person's idea of a good sermon is one that goes over his head and wakes his neighbor up.

The difference between the creationists and the evolutionists is whether you think Eve was given an apple by a snake or a banana by a monkey.

If psychics really want to do something to help the world, why don't they locate all those single socks that disappear from dryers?

Exorcist's motto: "With fiends like these, who needs entities?"

It's good for sinners to repent, but what makes them pent in the first place?

You hear about lots of folks who are superstitious, but never about somebody who's just plain ordinary stitious.

There is a higher power. They're called auto mechanics.

Some religious leaders refer to their congregation as their flock because they're always fleecing them.

Atheists don't have a prayer.

Don't you wish all those people trying to find themselves would get lost?

They say that eyes are the window to the soul, but that doesn't mean the mouth is the door to the brain.

And if everyone lit just one little candle, we'd all be at our wick's end.

Most folks would be more prepared to meet their Maker if they got a factory rebate.

The meek shall inherit the earth . . . if that's all right with the rest of you.

Cross training: seminary school.

Atheists' club: a nonprophet organization.

SHOW BIZ

They ought to expand the movie-rating system to include RS: Really Stinks.

Hollywood: marriage recycling center.

Modern movies contain so much bad language, you'd think they're being made by a bunch of irate golfers.

It took about fifty years for movies to go from silent to unspeakable.

In Hollywood, if you want to hear your calling, you phone in to your message machine.

Astronomy follows the stars by calculation, astrology by the zodiac, and Hollywood follows them by reading the tabloids.

Hollywood is based on the proposition that all movies are created equal to a sequel.

There may be other fish in the sea, but all the barracudas have crawled out and moved into Hollywood.

If talent is a gift, then a lot of today's stars must have been bribes.

In Hollywood, they think America is the home of the babes and the land of the Brie.

If you really want your ears pierced, try listening to rock and roll.

I suppose all those people in Hollywood constantly wear sunglasses because they're always looking on the bright side.

If idle minds are the devil's playground, then Hollywood must be his major amusement park.

What's so new about recycling trash? Gossip columnists have been doing it for years.

Even gossip columnists have their function in the garden of life. They like to dig up the dirt.

Did you hear about the actor who was so stupid that when his agent told him he had charisma, he went to see a dermatologist.

The reason movies no longer leave anything to the imagination is that the filmmakers don't have any.

Someone should tell those people in Hollywood that nobody's ship ever came in at a swimming pool.

Fire-eaters believe a mouth's attracted to a flame.

Ask a foolish question and you're probably a game-show host.

Pay dirt: steamy novelist's royalty check.

In Hollywood, people try to put their best face forward.

Permanent press: an invention of Hollywood.

Some things go without saying . . . but just try telling that to a gossip columnist.

TV newscasters used to need a degree in journalism. Now they need a degree in cosmetology.

Hollywood is always searching for new faces . . . that's why they have so many plastic surgeons out there.

Why do they still call them soap operas when they've gotten so dirty?

The reason so many TV shows and movies are cheesy is because of all the rats in Hollywood.

Did you hear about the doctor who gave the flu injection to the TV star? It was his only shot at show business.

He who laughs last will never get to sit with a studio audience.

Hear no evil, see no evil, speak no evil . . . and you'll never work for a celebrity magazine.

One thing's for sure, they don't call it pop music because your dad likes it.

The reason you don't see many torch singers around anymore is that they're always getting fired.

From the look of all these daytime talk shows, there's certainly no such thing as mind over patter.

What a comic calls his extra jokes: laughed-overs.

Hope springs eternal in the human breast, but in Hollywood hype springs eternal from the human breath.

America has become so voyeuristic, we're going to have to change it to "We, the peephole."

Some celebrities think they're photogenic when they're just overexposed.

Hollywood: the land of bilk and money.

Music videos: empty v.

The best part of a telepathic awards show: no long, loud speeches.

Movie buff: someone who remembers when Robert Young and Loretta Young were.

Hollywood starlets dress for sex-cess.

Photo finish: when paparazzi attend celebrity funerals.

And then there was the lady who thought *Jaws* was a training film for gossips.

Oxymoron: television actor.

Movie star: someone who struggles to get famous so she can complain about being recognized all the time.

If confession is good for the soul, then all those talk-show celebrities must be the most righteous people around.

If you can't say anything good about a person . . . you just qualified for a job on a tabloid newspaper.

Some performances are electrifying, and some are just powered by hot air.

Hollywood is very geometric: it's the home of love triangles and square movies.

History tends to repeat itself . . . that's why TV shows all those reruns.

Then there was the guy who robbed the movie theater because he wanted to break into show business.

Many doors were opened for him in Hollywood. Unfortunately, they were all marked "Exit."

Beverly Hills: where people pay too much so they can feel rich.

Movie star: someone who finds their place in the sun and then complains about the glare.

Never before have so many movie stars been paid so much to do so little. Perhaps they should act their wage.

Hollywood is very patriotic: lots of stars and bars.

TV may be a popular way to kill time, but these new shows make it look like assassination.

Gossip columnists cover a lot of ground spreading the dirt.

The difference between watching TV and dying is that with TV, other people's lives flash before your eyes.

Did you hear about the vampire who met the comedian and got into a jocular vein?

They call those TV shows "sitcoms" because the audience sits and gets comatose.

Some entertainers are real showstoppers . . . the others just know how to slow them down.

Movie stars used to air their dirty laundry. Now they're not wearing enough laundry to air.

Movies are getting so filthy, they should be rated by the department of sanitation.

If misery loves company, how come those people on the soap operas never get along?

Some of these entertainers on the comeback trail ought to be shown the go-away road.

Movies are so popular because it's the only place you can dream and eat at the same time.

It used to be you were famous if they wrote a book about you. Nowadays, you haven't made it unless you're a major motion picture and a line of designer jeans.

Hollywood has proved that nothing succeeds like excess.

In Hollywood, all the stars hire public-affairs consultants because their affairs are all so public.

Movie stars never forget their age . . . once they've decided what it's going to be.

Advice to stars: if nobody knows the troubles you've seen, you need a new publicist.

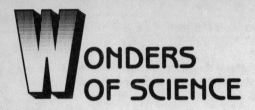

WONDERS OF SCIENCE

The worst part about the speed of light is it makes the mornings come awfully early.

Miracle drug: one the pharmacist only charges you ten bucks for.

If necessity actually was the mother of invention, do you really think we'd have liquid butter in a squeeze bottle?

City sidewalks: the grate outdoors.

Scientists crossed a pidgeon with a woodpecker. Now they have a bird that not only carries messages but knocks on doors, too.

Man is the lowest-cost nonlinear computer system capable of being mass produced by unskilled labor.

When remembering the greats of science, does the name Pavlov ring a bell?

How about the guy who crossed poison ivy with a four-leaf clover and got a rash of good luck?

What do you do when you see a bird on the endangered-species list eating a plant on the endangered species list?

Everyone wants their time in the sun . . . preferably before the ozone layer is gone.

What do you get when all the canisters of radioactive waste that have been dumped in the ocean finally corrode? Nuclear fishin'.

One good thing about the computer age . . . we can be wrong at astonishingly faster speeds.

Live wire: what you won't be if you touch one.

When you wish upon a star it takes two hundred million light-years to receive the request.

Did you hear about the new science that combines cosmology with cosmetology? It has to do with the makeup of the universe.

Entomologist etymologist: someone who studies bug languages.

If Darwin was right and fish crawled out of the sea, then the brass tacks of evolution is bass tracks.

Phonetics: the study of telephones, usually undertaken by teenagers.

What can you expect of a universe that started out as nothing but a lot of hot air?

For every action there is a reaction: the minute they invented windows, they had to invent shades.

You know it's time to clean out the refrigerator when your leftovers begin to look like science experiments.

Mathematicians' bakery: House of Pi's.

If Darwin wasn't right, how come it's so easy to make a monkey out of a man?

What we are going to have after we take all the ore from the earth: mined-over matter.

Hitch your wagon to a star . . . and you'll vaporize instantly.

Scientists say man is the only creature that can reason. That's because he's the only one who needs the excuses.

There's going to be a new technological revolution . . . led by all the people who can't figure out how to program their VCRs.

These new electronic computers are OK, but for most of us it will never replace the steam computer.

Sign on the door of a nuclear power plant: "Gone fission."

If technology is really making the world smaller, how come the phone bill keeps going up?

If your denim pants shrink in the wash, you end up with recessive jeans.

Modern times: when you finally walk on the sunny side of the street, and the ozone hole gets you.

We would know today who invented the wheel if they'd had a spokesperson.

By the time we're ready to get back to nature, nature may not be able to get back to us.

The science of casual wear: jeanetics.

Give some people an inch and they want the metric equivalent.

If only nature didn't abhor a vacuum, maybe our forests wouldn't be so dirty.

Studies show most docks collapse because of pier pressure.

Did you hear about the wealthy philanthropist who left all his money to earthquake research? He was generous to a fault.

Ornithologists are for the birds.

Just think: if Edison hadn't invented the electric light bulb, we'd all be working our computers by candlelight.

We may not know whether the chicken or the egg came first, but at the rate we're going we're sure to end up scrambled.

People may argue whether we came from the apes, but most agree that we're going to the dogs.

Scientists have discovered the only truly fireproof material is the boss's son.

The mind is an amazing thing: it can be totally empty and still not cave in.

Be thankful for skeptics. What if nobody had ever told Ben Franklin to go fly a kite, or Jacques Cousteau to go jump in a lake?

Genetics: the study of which parent's family is responsible for a teenager's behavior.

Evolution is just nature's way of trying to cover its mistakes.

When males pass on the gene for weak knees: the shins of the father are visited upon the son.

The reason it's taking scientists so long to map the human brain is all the dead ends and rest stops they've found along the way.

They once said computers would cut down paperwork. Now there's just as much paper, except you have to tear off those little perforated edges with the holes.

We'll never find intelligent life on other planets. If they're really intelligent, they'll avoid us.

Rock show: when geologists parade their wares.

According to scientists, there are only two species who would not upset the ecological balance by their elimination: rats and talk-show hosts.

Do you ever feel like this is the computer age and you're a hand-cranked mimeograph machine?

It's all very fine to be able to fly faster than the speed of sound, but what if you want to have a conversation?

Do you ever feel like you're stuck in the microchip revolution with nothing but a bowl of microdip?

Old statisticians never die, they just know when their number's up.

The thing that really separates us from the lower life-forms is our ability to use and enjoy small appliances.

Science is trying to figure out a way to turn garbage into fuel, and they'll probably succeed. After all, they're already using it to make TV shows.

If rocks aren't romantic, why is there carbon dating?

Modern technology requires millions of dollars to make things smaller and smaller, but laundries have been doing the same thing for years . . . free of charge.

Relativity: that's when the number of people who claim to be your relatives is in direct proportion to the number of dollars you have in the bank.

If mankind is so evolved, then why do we need lobster bibs?

People who say "The sky's the limit" are never going to get a job with NASA.

Mad scientist: one who's just had his federal grant taken away.

Now that we have digital clocks, we'll never be able to turn back the hands of time.

Petroleum actually comes from things like decomposed dinosaurs . . . proving there's no fuel like an old fuel.

Eternity: from the beginning to the end of the universe, or the time it takes to pay off your mortgage, whichever comes last.

We won't have to worry about polluting anymore if corporations keep moving overseas and the price of gas keeps going up.

LEGAL LIABILITIES

Some lawyers have a lot of class, and some lawyers just have a lot of class action.

There is a positive side to divorce. Lawyers need vacation homes too.

Lawyer: someone with both the gift of gab and the gift of grab.

These days, if you build a better mousetrap, the attorneys for the mice will slap an injunction on you.

Other people don't want to hear your troubles . . . unless, of course, they're litigation lawyers.

Lawyers do everything by the book . . . the bankbook.

Why don't they have combination doctor's/lawyer's offices, so you can spend all your money in one easy visit?

Talk is cheap . . . unless, of course, you're a lawyer.

These days, when the going gets tough, the tough call their lawyers.

Nowadays, if a genie gives you three wishes, you have to use one of them on a good lawyer to get you out of the other two.

There's a clothing store exclusively for attorneys . . . they specialize in lawsuits.

Never hire a lawyer who has the courage of your convictions.

Where there's a will there's a way . . . to stuff all your relatives into one lawyer's office for the reading.

There's a big market for exorcist/attorneys because possession is nine-tenths of the law.

Lawyer's motto: "To err is human; to litigate, the fine.

If there is such a thing as natural selection, how come we haven't evolved beyond lawyers?

What the cannibals called the lawyer: legal tender.

An apple a day may keep the doctor away, but a banana peel will always attract a couple of lawyers.

If crime doesn't pay, why are there so many lawyers?

If talk is cheap, how come lawyers charge so much?

Lawyers have to pass the bar only once . . . after that they can go in for a drink whenever they want to.

Lawyers: what kids who play pirate grow up to be.

Lawyer's wardrobe: lawsuit, legal briefs.

Property-litigation specialist: da fence lawyer.

Divorce lawyer: someone who thinks it's better to have loved and won.

Lawyers are to clients as farmers are to cows: they milk you for all you've got.

Court case: the one that holds the lawyer's tennis racket.

REAL JOBS

Watch repairman: someone you see when you don't have the time.

Chimney sweep: a man whose job soots him.

If you're tired of living life in the fast lane, get a job at the post office.

Most people don't want to be trash collectors because they're always down in the dumps.

Forgery artist: someone who does bad by following a good example.

When tunnelers dig into each other's paths: meeting of the mines.

School bus driver: someone who thought they liked children.

Waiter: someone who believes that money grows on trays.

Ever notice how geologists are always finding fault?

Cobblers work on a shoestring budget.

Cosmetologists have to take makeup exams.

Grocers: people who invested in the market.

Candlemakers are often at their wick's end.

The coast guard; where they separate the men from the buoys.

If you want to stay ahead of the crowd, become a tour guide.

The hardest part about owning a bar is you have so few upstanding customers.

Obviously, lumber yards believe money grows on trees.

Competition is so tough these days, the only people who can afford to throw in the towel are linen salesmen.

The real reason they pay chefs at those fancy restaurants so much is to compensate them for having to wear those silly hats.

Hairdressers need to get on the right wavelength.

A nuclear-missile silo is one place where you don't want a guy with hands-on experience.

Woodcutter's store: chopping mall.

What do teachers and highway construction workers have in common? They both grade on a curve.

Locomotive engineers get on-the-job train-ing.

When postmen bundle letters: mail bonding.

Taxidermist: a skin doctor for cabbies.

Loggers like to go on chopping sprees.

If you really want to get ahead in your work, become a hairdresser.

The customer is always right . . . unless you run a taxi service, in which case the customer is always left.

Sweater manufacturers are just trying to pull the wool over our eyes.

The only ones guaranteed to move up in their jobs anymore are high-rise construction workers.

A great actor can bring tears to our eyes. But then, so can an auto mechanic.

You haven't really sunk as low as you can until you take up deep-sea diving.

Oil drilling: a boring profession.

Air-traffic controllers have friends in high places.

A barber is a man of many parts.

Prospector: golden retriever.

It's not always a good idea to whistle while you work . . . particularly for wine tasters and mimes.

Boxers have the gift of the jab.

Submarine crewmen hang out in a lot of dives.

Chicken farmer: cluck watcher.

Power lunch: when electric linemen eat on the job.

Bakers have flour power.

When circus animal trainers take a book break: reading between the lions.

Show me a sailor who needs new electrical power for his boat and I'll show you a salt and battery.

The difference between being a gambler and a waiter in a Chinese restaurant: one rolls the dice, the other doles the rice.

Bell ringers are always at the end of their rope.

With the economy the way it is, the only way to have a bright future is if you manufacture lamps.

It's a competitive world. If you don't get fired up, you just get fired.

The difference between a solitary boatman and a banker: one floats alone and the other floats a loan.

Complaint department: whine merchant.

Pity the poor bracelet designers. Their careers are always out on a limb.

Bakery pinup: roll model.

Window installers take great panes to please their customers.

You should always keep your chin up in times of adversity . . . unless, of course, you're a prizefighter.

It's hard to be an electrician unless you have good connections.

Constructive criticism: when architects argue.

Did you hear about the country judge who fed his pigs nothing but court documents? He was trying to take the law into his own hams.

Pipe dreams: when plumbers sleep.

When pearl fishermen drink, they assign a designated diver.

Give a gardener an inch and he'll take a yard.

Shoe repairmen do a lot of sole-searching.

You don't know what it's really like to feel light-headed until you've worn a miner's helmet.

You know all about power dressing if you're a lineman for the electric company.

Nature abhors a vacuum; that's why it's so hard to be a vacuum-cleaner salesman.

Perfume sales training operates on the in-scentive program.

Oceanographers are deep sinkers.

The retread business is tiring work.

If you really want to make your mark in the world, become a tattooist.

The first thing they learn in the police academy is that the Miranda Act has nothing to do with wearing fruit on your head.

Then there was the worker in the orange-juice factory who was fired because he couldn't concentrate.

If you really want your career to be rising, buy a bakery.

If you really want your work to bear fruit, try selling apples on the corner.

Lots of businesses are making cutbacks . . . particularly dress manufacturers.

Bakery supplier: dough-to-dough salesman.

Not every career has a future in it, but at least being a florist has a fuchsia in it.

Obituary writers always get the last word.

Swiss-cheese makers have a holier-than-thou attitude.

Did you hear about the gangster's son who became a cop, so he took after his father's side of the family?

When bricklayers retire, they throw in the trowel.

It takes a lot of training to be an engineer . . . and it takes a lot of boating to be a sailor.

Besides Sherlock Holmes, the only person who really looks more distinguished with a pipe is a plumber.

Did you hear about the electrician who got tired of eating jelly so he started alternating currant?

Bad career planning: a ski instructor in Kansas.

Automatic teller: the town gossip.

Chimney sweeps get lousy wages . . . which only proves that grime doesn't pay.

Hairstylists are always paying their dues by spraying their dos.

Everybody's on a schedule these days. Even lumberjacks have to log their time.

Milkman's memoirs: dairy diary.

Watch repair: apart-time job.

If knowledge is power, how come teachers get such low pay?

Weight lifter's motto: "No pain, no gain." Farmer's motto: "No plain, no grain."

Traffic cop's motto: "Seek and ye shall fine."

You don't really know what job security is until you're right-hand man to a guy named Lefty.

How about the fisherman whose wife thought he was going deaf but he was just hard of herring.

Ancient warfare was fought with men swinging clubs, stalking through the fields, and shouting terrible oaths. So is modern golf.

Clowns get the fruits of their labors by slipping on banana peels.

A pearl diver's profession works backwards: they start at the top and work their way to the bottom.

Prospector comedian: gold card.

In this fast-paced world, the only people with time on their hands are watchmakers.

Astronomers are a lot like press agents: they both make their living off the stars.

Haberdashers are always trying to go over your head.

These days, the only sure way to be rolling in the dough is if you're a baker.

Siberian jailer: cold turnkey.

One-man butcher shop: where they also serve, who stand and weigh it.

Auto mechanics come from the school of hard knocks.

Lots of newsmen can break a story; the trick is putting it together again.

Sweater makers are a tight-knit group.

Post office graffiti: "Help stamp out philatelists."

These days, if you want to push the envelope, you'd better be a test pilot or a postal worker.

Show me a man who's done the same job in a furniture factory for twenty years and I'll show you a chair man of the bored.

Stockroom work is very uplifting.

Translators are always just giving lip service.

Then there was the boatbuilder who showed his kid his wood supplies and said, "Someday, son, all this will be oars."

The difference between an optimist and a vampire killer: one counts his blessings, the other blesses his counts.

Then there was the shepherd who sang, "I Got Plenty of Mutton."

For a cobbler, shoe repair is the sole means of support.

Clothes make the man . . . unless you're a tailor, in which case man makes the clothes.

The difference between being a prospector and going to the butcher: one stakes his claim, the other claims his steaks.

They now have computer doctors for computers that catch a "virus" . . . or get a slipped disk.

Watchmakers' billboard: sign of the times.

Even carpenters have their vices.

Seamstress: the original "material girl."

The only people who are really dressed to kill are hunters.

Did you hear about the doctor who treated the swim team? He made them sit in the wading room.

Some people just aren't cut out to be swordsmen.

Did you hear about the crooked electrician who was light-fingered?

We all have to pay the piper . . . particularly when the plumbing springs a leak.

When old clockmakers die, it takes a long time to wind up their estates.

Casino owner: vice president.

A lot of folks don't like to hear four-letter words . . . like "work."

People who rest on their laurels should stop sitting on shrubbery and get back to work.

Computers haven't cut down on mistakes, it's just harder now to place the blame.

Efficiency expert: someone who uses charts and graphs to tell you what you already knew.

Intuition: that which allows a boss to find fault before you've done anything wrong.

These days, the only people who can operate on a shoestring budget are shoestring salesmen.

The worst part about out-of-town conventions is they prove how expendable you are to the office.

The best way to keep your job is to let the boss carefully explain how to do something, then quietly do it the right way.

Dictation: where you recite a lot of words to your secretary that you can't spell.

Some people get to the top only because they got stuck in back of the elevator.

You know it's time to look for a new job when the company applies for status as a nonprofit organization.

Born executive: one whose father owns the business.

Computers will never replace humans until they learn how to laugh at the boss's jokes.

The only reason that computers can do more work than people is they don't have to stop to answer the phone.

Most bosses don't mind if you march to the beat of a different drummer, as long as you speed up the beat.

Then there was the misguided fortune-cookie company that decided to expand its business and put fortunes in ice cream and pudding.

Redundancy of the year: "working mother."

When all is said and nothing done . . . the committee meeting is over.

Executive: somebody who keeps their eye on the ball while dropping it.

They say it's a jungle out there, but in real jungles, when they have lunch, you're it.

Perfect gift for a surly boss: an executive chew toy.

When your boss says it's time to start pooling your resources, you know he's getting ready to do the backstroke.

It's hard to keep your chin up when you have to keep your nose to the grindstone.

If you want to be in a business that makes some noise, open a nursery school for crying out loud.

As you climb the ladder of success, have you noticed the boss's son taking the elevator?

Newest business combination: happy-hour bar with an auto-body shop.

If at first you don't succeed, the other guy gets the promotion.

Times do change. Power dressing used to be a suit of armor and a lance.

If you keep people in the dark, they can't tell if you're asleep on the job.

People who let themselves get too tied up with business should remember the same thing used to happen to horse thieves.

Behind every successful man stands a bunch of amazed co-workers.

Usually when businesses advertise, "Position available," the position is either shoulder-to-the-wheel or nose-to-the-grindstone.

Some folks want to set the world on fire and some folks just want to sell you the fuel.

Conference: where people take off from work to talk about working.

You can't climb to the top of the ladder without getting a few splinters.

Behind every successful man stands somebody ready to push him out of the way.

These days, when the going gets tough everybody calls in sick.

People who think they're big shots usually end up getting fired.

The only thing more overrated than Mom's apple pie is owning your own business.

You know it's going to be a bad week when your boss mails you the want ads.

If at first you do succeed, it's probably your father's business.

Business-meeting tip: when making a point, make sure it's not with your head.

The best way to get ahead is to work hard; the second-best way is for your employees to work hard.

One-product merchandiser: a single-sell organism.

It's hard to be a team player when the boss is always throwing you curves.

Tied up at the office: when bankers get robbed.

There are lots of people as honest as the day is long. They're called cat burglars.

The best way to learn tolerance is to have a boss who thinks he's funny.

Most people don't mind going to work. It's the working itself they don't like.

If you can keep your composure when crises occur, you must have a fall guy.

If you want your business to prosper, always hire optimists for the sales department and pessimists for the credit department.

If you can see the writing on the wall, you probably run a day-care center.

Paleontologists make no bones about their profession.

THE GETTING
OF WISDOM

Food for thought: catering a philosophers' convention.

Maybe we should make the teaching profession a branch of the armed forces so they can qualify for combat pay.

Kids go to college so they can graduate and join the work farce.

The best thing about an education is it lets you be confused about everything on a more sophisticated level.

People who live in glass libraries shouldn't throw tomes.

Kids are doing so poorly in college now that most of them think an English major is a British officer.

If you really want to see low interest rates, check out the attentiveness of students at a lecture.

Bar exam: the final test at saloon school.

If language is a vehicle of thought, then a lot of people are hauling empty boxcars.

Remember, if your parents can't afford to send you to medical school you can always will your body to science and get there eventually.

Some people go to college to drink from the well of knowledge, and others go to drain the dregs of fraternity.

Nodding acquaintance: schoolmate at naptime.

They ought to have library police for ticketing speed readers.

Teaching may not pay much, but at least it's a job with class.

And if you go to music school, they assign you hum work.

Light reading: seeing what the wattage on the bulb is.

Colleges used to produce men of letters. Now it's hard to find anyone who even writes postcards.

Why don't we get teenagers to teach in our universities? After all, they're the experts on everything.

The problem with sending a kid to college is that you have to send all your money along, too.

The brain is an amazing instrument. It works perfectly up until the teacher asks you a question.

Highbrow: someone who's read all the best book titles.

Genius: someone too smart to make a living.

Did you hear about the agriculture major voted most likely to sack seed?

Language is funny. Just when you think you know the meaning of the word "stupid," someone comes along and redefines it.

Most people know what real class is . . . it's a room with about thirty kids imprisoned in it.

Grade-school teachers' motto: "Nothing succeeds like recess."

If we don't improve our schools, every kid in America will get a free education . . . free of any knowledge whatsoever.

You know they are getting soft on education when they just assign the movie versions of the classic books for homework.

Charm school: where witches go to learn their spells.

One reason experience is such a good teacher is it doesn't allow any dropouts.

What's the point in taking speed-reading courses if they don't teach you how to speed-think?

People who go to cooking school really know what it means to cram for exams.

Anyone who thinks there's no more prayer in public schools should listen closely to the students' mumbling before final exams.

The difference between a fertile mind and a dirty mind depends on what's planted in it.

If experience is such a great teacher, how come you never get to graduate?

The world's gotten so competitive, college athletes are now required to go to class.

You know someone's educated when they can say exactly what they think without anyone having the slightest idea what they're saying.

If you really want to be a man of letters, change your name to "occupant."

A wise person collects books because he knows it's best to put something away for a brainy day.

College administrators would like to have more football players with passing ability.

With college prices what they are now, you might as well just buy your kids their own business and save some cash.

A lot of reading can be dull, but cookbooks are always full of stirring passages.

Sign on a school bulletin board: "Free knowledge. Bring your own container."

Fraternities are very ecological. They're always trying to keep the wild life from becoming extinct.

A student bemoaned his astronomy class, claiming the subject was over his head.

THE SPORTING LIFE

How many men would continue to watch sports if they had to run on a treadmill to keep the TV going?

Golf handicap: when you're playing with the boss.

Golf club: hand-powered weed-eater.

The main reason there aren't more elephant hunters is that the decoys are so heavy.

The way some people play golf, the green flags ought to be lowered to half-mast.

Best way to stop a runaway horse: bet on it.

Golf used to be a rich man's sport. Now it has millions of poor players.

The perfect reducing machine has been invented. It's so expensive, you have to starve to keep up the payments.

Next time someone tells you nothing is impossible, ask him to dribble a football.

This year's college football lineup looks so bad they may actually have to use students on the team.

Height isn't really a requirement for basketball, just as long as you're tall enough so that your ears pop when you sit down.

A horseshoe is a symbol of good luck, particularly if it's on the right horse.

Golf is like love. If you don't take it seriously it's no fun, and if you do take it seriously it'll break your heart.

The real reason mountain climbers tie themselves together is to keep the sensible ones from going home.

There's one big difference between learning to drive a car and learning to play golf: when you are learning golf, you don't hit anything.

Never fall in love with a tennis player. "Love" means nothing to them.

We all have mountains in life to climb . . . unless, of course, you can afford the ski lift.

If you scuba dive off Corpus Christi, there's nothing certain but depth in Texas.

Let's face it, the only ones who can really throw their weight around are bodybuilders.

Old skiers never die . . . they just get over the hill.

Life is like basketball: some people score points while others just dribble.

Everybody's allowed an occasional failure . . . unless you're a sky diver.

Bow tie: archery contest where nobody wins.

What's the big deal about big-game hunting? Who wants to shoot a Monopoly board, anyway?

Did you hear about the student pilot who took a crash course in flying?

Sportsmanship: a fishing boat.

Show me an Arabian prince playing dice and I'll show you a sheikh, rattle, and roll.

Wrestling fans give the sport the best jeers of their lives.

In croquet, like life, there's no rest for the wicket.

This year, when the first baseball of the season was thrown, the cry was "Pay ball!"

Vampire contest: neck-and-neck competition.

For some people, recycling means the return trip of a bike race.

People who don't like duck hunting will always try to duck hunting.

These days, the only way someone will go to bat for you is if you own a baseball team.

Bull fight: two guys arguing about who caught the biggest fish last summer.

We don't want to accuse sports figures of being uptight, but one out of every two football players is defensive.

People who are really on the ball are usually at the bottom of a pile of football players.

Some people still throw themselves into their work . . . Olympic divers, for instance.

Olympic swimmers have a way of pooling their resources.

Lots of people go to the racetrack looking for a lucky break—and end up broke.

Parachutists jump for joy.

The easiest way to be good at golf is to be bad at arithmetic.

Man of letters: college tri-athlete.

At least if you're a balloonist, people look up to you.

Poor loser: somebody who played for money.

There are two good things about skiing: you don't have to work your way to the top, and no one's disappointed in you when you've hit bottom.

For some people, the only kick they'll ever get out of life is a punt.

It isn't whether you win or lose. It's whether you made the referee miserable.

Hunting would be more a sport if they gave the deer AK-47s with telescopic sights.

Baseball is the national pastime, mainly because we like to see other guys striking out.

Contortionists are so considerate; they're always bending over backwards for people.

If time waits for no one, how come they're always stopping the clock at football games?

A sign from above: when skywriters fly.

Running the numbers: contestants in a marathon race.

It's taken us a million years to come from swinging in the trees to swinging on the fairways.

The only ones who go to the school of hard knocks anymore are boxers.

Scuba divers are always putting on airs.

Life is like a football game . . . and the position most of us play is drawback.

Sports figures aren't what they used to be, but at least you can still look up to basketball players.

Forethought: when golfers daydream.

Not all aspects of navigation are ironclad; sometimes it's an either-oar situation.

In football, the best offense is usually the fans yelling at the opposing team.

You know you've got a lousy baseball team when they start selling hot dogs to go in the fifth inning.

The worst thing about being a good sport is you have to lose to prove it.

IN THE SPIRIT OF THE SEASON

Whoever said you can't fool all of the people all of the time has never tried to assemble a kid's toy on Christmas Eve.

Life is like buying a Christmas gift: as soon as you begin to like it, it's time to wrap it up.

You can dream all you want about a white Christmas; it's still going to leave you in the red.

The trouble with Thanksgiving dinner is you eat one and five days later you're hungry again.

Father's Day advice: never look a gift tie in the mirror.

There are two kinds of Christmas gifts: those you don't like, and those you don't get.

The three stages of Man: he believes in Santa; he doesn't believe in Santa; he is Santa.

Red and green are the traditional Christmas colors . . . representing the green you spend before Christmas and the red you're in after.

Christmas: a contract of happiness you make with your children containing a hidden Claus.

Once again, Christmas decked us all with fiscal folly.

Unfortunately, too many people celebrate the Fourth with a fifth.

When it comes to birthday parties, there's no time like the presents.

Thanksgiving is the day on which all people are thankful they're not turkeys.

Once a year we settle around the family hearth and pick up the book that makes our holiday cheer possible . . . the checkbook.

Ah, an old-fashioned Christmas! Chestnuts roasting in the microwave, creditors nipping at your toes!

Christmas comes but once a year, but the bills keep coming through all seasons.

For all you who made New Year's resolutions: today is the first day of the rest of your lies.

Thanksgiving is the time of year when we're thankful to be well off enough to eat until we get sick.

April 1: If you think this is April Fool's Day, just wait until April 15.

Thanksgiving is a time when turkeys turn from gobblers to gobblees.

Christmas is a magical time . . . it's when all your money does a disappearing act.

With the kind of gifts people are giving nowadays, Santa's going to have to change his name to Yves St. Claus.

Most New Year's resolutions are taken with a grain . . . usually whiskey or beer.

The citizens have shown they're thankful this Thanksgiving by electing a turkey for president.

Show me a lawn chair on St. Patrick's Day and I'll show you Patty O'Furniture.

International Thanksgiving: turkey and grease.

ART FOR ART'S SAKE

The difference between an actor and a player piano: one plays roles, the other plays rolls.

People who wed poets marry for better or verse.

Then there was the artist who worked himself to death. He painted himself into a coroner.

If Shakespeare were alive today, he might write for a medium other than the stage: "TV or not TV, that is the question."

Musicians' wills are seldom contested, since they are all of sound mind.

Nobody likes to do home improvements. Even Michelangelo didn't want to paint the Sistine Chapel ceiling.

Writer's block: that object attached to a writer's shoulders.

When painters throw a fit: tempera tantrum.

Musicians always strive to become noteworthy.

If music is the language of the soul, then sound effects must be the language of the heel.

People who write poetry immediately after getting up in the morning are just going from bed to verse.

Graffiti is nothing but a lot of off-the-wall comments.

Prestidigitation: the hands of fake.

Miniaturists are small-minded people.

Then there was the tattooed man who favored numbers so that his friends could count on him.

When Pinocchio met his maker, he found out he was just a chip off the old block.

The horns of a dilemma: when a brass band loses its arrangements.

World's two shortest books: *Fun Dictators* and *Cats Who Swim*.

You can always tell a rich drummer by his status cymbals.

Best-selling author: one who is always having his writes read.

Show me a conference where not a word is spoken and I'll show you a meeting of the mimes.

Did you hear about the pasta chef who starting playing in the bar because they liked his noodling on the piano?

Of all the money invested in opera, the best spent is on a pair of earplugs.

Give some people enough rope and they'll start doing macramé.

Ballet's all right. At least it keeps you on your toes.

One look at some of these modern sculptures is enough to know they've been done by chiselers.

There must be a lot of music haters out there . . . there's been a lot of complaining about sax and violins on PBS TV.

B.C.: before comedy, in prehysteric times.

Budding artist: a painter of floral arrangements.

Other ages produced period furniture. Nowadays we have furniture that produces only question marks.

Country classic: Bach in the saddle.

Did you hear about the still-life painter who peeled all the apples because he wanted his work to bare fruit?

Prehysteric art: before the NEA became censors.

Sewing bee: a stitchin' time.

Taking notes can always help your work . . . particularly if you take them from dead composers.

Some people will support culture only when they start selling art by the pound.

When horn players just won't stop: saxual harassment.

Maybe children should be seen and not heard, but mimes should be neither.

The engraver's art is like a dog pointing: attention to de-tail.

It's not the big-city symphonies we hate . . . it's the random violins.

Everyone can carry a tune . . . it's just a question of how far.

Sex cymbal: what drummers hit at strip joints.

The school of mime went bankrupt . . . word just never got around.

When someone is said to have an artistic temperament, it means they're too old to spank.

You know a book is a success when everybody pretends they've read it.

STORMY WEATHER

Summer: these are the times that fry men's soles.

Weatherman's motto: to air is humid.

Every cloud has a silver lining . . . but only if you're getting paid as a TV weatherman.

Into every life some rain must fall, but nobody told us about all the drips.

Everybody talks about the weather, but how many people go out and buy barometers?

This is the time of year when a lot of people go ice fishing . . . in their highball glasses.

So Humpty Dumpty had a great fall. What about the rest of his year?

Some people are like snow: they storm in and act like flakes.

In summer, time flies, but it's also the flies' time.

Heat makes objects expand and cold makes them contract. That's why the days are longer in summer and shorter in winter.

Weathermen all have their heads in the clouds.

Summer is the time when Americans exercise one of their basic constitutional rights . . . the right to bare arms.

Sign on a ski resort: "There's no business like snow business."

With warm weather just around the corner, bathing suits should be really taking off this year.

Into each life some rain must fall, but Seattle must be taking the rap for the rest of us.

Summer's the time when you wonder what makes a dog tick.

Spring: that wonderful time when farmers and golfers begin to do their plowing.

Into each life some rain must fall . . . usually on weekends.

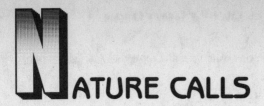NATURE CALLS

Spring is when you spend your time trying to get your lawn started. Summer is when you spend your time trying to get it to stop.

If dogs are so dumb, how come they stay at home sleeping while their masters go to work?

If owls are so smart, why don't they get on the day shift?

All gardeners believe what goes down must come up.

The real secret of having a green thumb is a willingness to get brown knees.

Sign in a florist shop: "With fronds like these, who needs anemones?"

By the time you stop and smell the roses, somebody's just spread out the fertilizer.

A bird in the hand may be worth two in the bush, but a bird in the cage is less messy.

A rose by any other name wouldn't cost twenty bucks a dozen.

The early bird catches the worm, and I say he can have it.

There's this to say about chicken noodle soup: if the chicken had used his noodle, he wouldn't be in the soup.

Just remember, the chicken who rules the roost today can get roasted tomorrow.

Hamster: a gangster pig.

Smart dog: a contradiction in terms, like honest politician.

Mountain greenery: fronds in high places.

When winged rodents laugh: batroom humor.

And if you're a bird, talk is cheep.

Bunny hops: rabbit beer.

Did you ever wonder whether pigs go through a mud-life crisis?

Every dog may have its day, but chances are he'll sleep right through it.

Down time: molting season for geese.

You can always recognize old rabbits by the gray hares.

Fast food: when lions hunt gazelle.

A bird in the hand is worth putting on gloves for.

If cats really do have nine lives, maybe they should send all the fat cats to fight the wars.

Barhopping: saloon for rabbits.

Pet peeve: when cats and dogs get angry.

Fly ball: a dance for bugs.

Trust a bird to always give a cheep compliment.

What you call a perpetual beaver colony: eternal dam nation.

Some dogs are tough . . . they can lick everyone in the family.

Bird dog: a woof in cheep's clothing.

If someone tells you the world is going to the cats, they're probably kitten you.

If you really want to lead a stable life, marry a horse.

If all birds of a feather did was flock together, you wouldn't need so much newspaper for the bottom of the cage.

Insecticide: when bugs kill themselves.

Canine jewelry can give your dog a new leash on life.

Hopscotch: when kangaroos drink.

Porcupine: animal acupuncture.

Dog owners know the beast things in life are flea.

Barnyard novel: *Life on the Lamb: When Sheep Go Baaad.*

Anyone who thinks they work like a dog has never owned one.

Giraffe family reunion: necks of kin.

Advice to canines who can't find a hydrant or a tree: get a lawn, little doggie.

Florist delivery truck: someone who stops to sell the roses.

Sign on a deer dormitory: "The buck stops here."

What's the big deal about people who get their dogs to talk? None of them have anything worthwhile to say.

When a horse gets married, they throw a bridle shower.

What's all this about animal rights? Most animals don't know their left from their right.

The latest for security-conscious people: digital watchdogs.

Lambs and sheep have mutton in common.

Florist shop: the stalk market.

If you don't like feeling down in the mouth, stop kissing geese.

If you really want the fur to fly, send your dog on an airplane trip.

The real reason a dog is man's best friend is that they don't understand a word you're saying.

Tickling the ivories: when elephants floss.

Doghouse: covered waggin'.

Homing pidgeon: bird with agoraphobia.

You can never trust a pig . . . they're full of baloney.

You can't make a silk purse out of a sow's ear, but you might be able to make a couple bucks selling an earless pig.

Power plant: a vegetable on steroids.

There's more than one way to skin a cat, but who really wants to know?

Dog is man's best friend. That doesn't say much for a man's intellectual level.

When the cat's away, the mice put on the dog.

It never fails that a swarm of insects are waiting for you whenever you go outside for a little recreation. In other words, flies time when you're having fun.

Judging from the way stables smell, you can lead a horse to water but you can't make him bathe.

Petroleum: a school where they teach dogs to roll over.

What's so special about being wise as an owl? They stay up all night and they're always putting themselves out on a limb.

When birds of a feather flock together, you'd better stay out from underneath them.

When it comes to horses, the neighs have it.

Bull behind a tapestry: when you can't see the taurus for the frieze.

Cat: beast of birdin'.

Sign on a dog pound: "Used curs."

Dairy diary: moo memoirs.

Beaver community: village of the dammed.

Best way to have pen pals without ever writing a letter: be a pig.

Animal husbandry: when a frat boy gets married.

Bicoastal dog story: *A Tail of Two Cities.*

Noisy birdwatchers: people who cry fowl.

Spelling bee: a literate insect.

What one ox said to the other: "The yoke's on us."

Porcupines may not be very popular animals, but they do have their points.

Did you hear about the giraffe race? It was neck-and-neck all the way.

Vanishing cream: when cows go on low-cholesterol diets.

Duck call: a real quack-up.

Bull dozer: sleeping steer.

Bridal path: the road where you lead horses . . . or bachelors.

Catalog: scratching post for felines.

Dogs in the new housing developments are always barking up the wrong stump.

When angry bees collect nectar: cross-pollination.

A musical insect: Gnat King Cole.

Groundhogs are living on burrowed time.

If you don't think money grows on trees, just see how much it costs to get one pruned.

The nice thing about horses is some engineer doesn't redesign them every year and make yours obsolete.

THE SOCIAL ORDER

Behind every successful antique shop there's a junk store.

The tighter some people become, the looser their tongues get.

He who laughs last is the guy who was intending to tell the same joke.

Steering committee: when you have two backseat drivers.

Most people who are aimless don't have the ammunition anyway.

People who lose their heads have a tendency to misplace lots of other small things.

Gossip: mouth-to-mouth recitation.

The best way to spoil a good discussion is to include someone who knows what he's talking about.

The next time a Yankee criticizes the South, just ask him if he ever heard of anyone retiring and going north.

Blunt people always come to the point.

You can always tell the host at a party. He's the one who keeps looking at his watch.

No matter how small a town is, you can always find someone to give you wrong directions.

A broad-minded person is one who can see both points of view . . . the wrong one, and his own.

Good conversationalist: someone who shares your opinions.

Who says chivalry is dead? When a lady drops something, most guys will kick it back to her.

It's not so easy to get a parking ticket. First you have to find a parking space.

Have you ever noticed how all the great historical events occurred right next door to souvenir shops?

Lots of people have the gift of gab; so few know how to wrap it up.

Friend: someone who's always around when he needs you.

Gossip: letting the chat out of the bag.

Some people are waiting for their ship to come in, and some people are just waiting for their bus to show up.

Some people can read you like a book review.

Just when you think you've got the big picture, someone changes the channel.

As we march toward the Hall of Fame, most of us get stuck in the vestibule of obscurity.

Beware of people with pressing engagements; they're probably just taking someone to the cleaners.

In this country, you're innocent until you're proven guilty . . . or until you publish your memoirs, whichever comes first.

Some people see their future looming before them, and others see it weaving.

Some people you can read like a book . . . a comic book.

Some people go out of their way for you when you just wish they'd get out of your way.

By the time you learn the ropes, you're fit to be tied.

If you really want to claw your way to the top, buy a scratching post.

Illegal aliens: convicts from outer space.

It's funny how people who insist on giving you food for thought always offer so many helpings.

Beware of folks who say they'll go to bat for you . . . they're just as likely to use it on you.

Opportunist: someone who, when the world goes to the dogs, becomes a veterinarian.

The only way some people can get on a roll is with training wheels.

"The first shall be last and the last shall be first": When too many people save places for their friends in the movie line.

Do you ever get the feeling life is a Cadillac showroom and you're a pair of fuzzy dice?

Some people have wits like a razor . . . flat and disposable.

As we go down life's highway, most of us now wish we'd consulted a travel agent first.

For some people the only way to jog their memory is to run at the mouth.

The closest some people get to back-to-the-land is throwing dirt about their neighbors.

Some towns are still innocent enough that the only shady business dealings involve window treatments.

No man is an island, but most of us feel like outlying suburbs.

Most people are a lot like coffee . . . they're either perky or drips.

People who constantly shoot off their mouths are usually loaded with blanks.

Some people write their legacy on the sands of time with a tube of suntan lotion.

It wouldn't be so bad being led out to pasture if they didn't give you all that bull when they did it.

Have you ever noticed that when someone's called the toast of the town, it's usually because they have a lot of bread and are from the upper crust?

Ambidextrous people are very evenhanded.

For those consumed by self-pity, crying is a water sport.

Usually, when someone tells you to "play ball," they want to use your head as the ball.

People who make insulting remarks believe the best defense is a good offense.

It's not rush-hour traffic you want to avoid, it's lush-hour traffic.

For some people, life is an enchanted dance close to the flame; for others, it's a polka next to the heating pad.

He's a man of many parts. Unfortunately, none of them fit together.

Do you ever feel like life is a lush garden, and you've only been hired to pull the weeds?

Not only is it a jungle out there, but swinging vines are only available on a time-share basis.

We can soon expect a salt shortage . . . considering all the things that now have to be taken with a grain of it.

You know you're not welcome when you try to spread a little sunshine and people start slathering on the sunblock.

The difference between a beach bum and a feudal landowner in the morning: one yells, "Surf's up!" and the other yells, "Serfs, up!"

You know you live in a rough neighborhood when, instead of asking what time it is, people just take your watch.

Do you ever get the feeling that life is a great tapestry to paint upon, and all you've got is a nubby crayon?

Lots of people are self-made, but not everyone reads the instructions for assembly.

Some people get all the breaks . . . while the rest of us just get the sprains.

Do you ever get the feeling life is a jet-plane ride and you're a piece of lost luggage?

The problem with having a mind like a steel trap is that you can get metal block.

Most people never make the same mistake twice because there are so many new ones to make.

When Marie Antoinette said, "Let them eat cake," she must have been thinking about their just desserts.

Elevator shoes: for people too lazy to put their foot in their mouth without help.

Some people are ashamed of their past and others just write best-sellers.

Do you ever get the feeling life is a garage sale and you're a moose head?

Life is like a restaurant: what you want isn't on the menu, and what you get shouldn't be.

Maturity: that process where, instead of being full of promise, you're full of excuses.

The art of conversation is tricky; it's a short distance from "more ironic" to "I'm moronic."

When the chips are down, you might as well get the dip out, too.

Some people get brainstorms . . . but most of us are fair to partly cloudy with scattered showers.

Some people are men of letters and others are just bulk-rate postage.

Have you ever noticed that whenever somebody gives you a snow job, you're the one left to shovel it up?

If these are the times that try men's souls, isn't it time to convict the heels?

Most folks think the way to rise above the crowd is to be full of hot air.

If fools rush in where angels fear to tread, why do they still call it Los Angeles?

Ever notice how when something's tailored to your needs you end up getting taken to the cleaners?

Tact: when you bite the hand that feeds you and pretend you're having finger sandwiches.

All the world's a stage, and most of us are bit-part players.

Do you ever feel like life is just a bowl of cherries, and you're a brussels sprout?

Everyone starts out wanting to set the world on fire and ends up settling for a backyard barbecue.

The true measure of success is how inferior you make your friends feel.

People used to be judged by know-how . . . now it's know-who.

Funny how most people throw in the towel just about the time they're all wet.

Some things bring a lump to your throat because they're hard to swallow.

Convincing argument: one in which your opponent cons you without your vincing.

It's easier to live up to a good name than to live down a bad reputation.

Sure it's lonely at the top, but it beats having to wait in line.

The best reason to wrestle with your conscience is so you won't get beat up by a bad reputation.

Nobody's perfect, but some people could use major renovation.

It used to be we couldn't see the forest for the trees; now we can't see the forest for the condos.

Life is like a smorgasbord: there are so many things to choose from, but by the time you get to the table all that's left are creamed corn and brussels sprouts.

We all occasionally wonder what it would be like to be in someone else's shoes . . . but nobody wants to be in someone else's socks.

Some people march to a different drummer . . . the kind that keeps them going around in circles.

If everyone wants to find their place in the sun, why are there so many tanning salons?

The difference between a discussion and an argument is whether you're winning it or not.

Ever notice how people who expect you to "play ball" are always the ones holding the bat?

Do you feel like you lead a dog's life and everyone else is a flea?

Most of the people who want to be in the limelight are actually lemons.

Don't you wish all those people with get-up-and-go would get up and go?

Why be hard on yourself when your friends are so willing to do it for you?

The only way some folks can get peace of mind is to give others a piece of their mind.

Just about the time you see the light at the end of the tunnel, you realize it's an oncoming train.

Life is like the movies: you're constantly in the dark, making projections.

They broke the mold when they made some people. With others, it just got severely bent.

Social grace: when you start out on the right foot instead of putting it in your mouth.

It's better to start snubbing people when you're a nobody; that way nobody can say you've changed when you're a success.

Beware of people who want to put you on a pedestal . . . they might be raising pidgeons.

The road to success isn't easy . . . particularly with all the "Yield" signs along the way.

Do you ever get the feeling that life is just one long party . . . one to which you weren't invited?

Some people are as honest as the day is long . . . a winter's day.

Some people have milestones in their lives, and others just have millstones.

If at first you don't succeed, try to look surprised.

For some people life is a veil of tears, and for others life is a trail of beers.

There's a big difference between marching to a different drummer and having no sense of rhythm.

You're either living up to your reputation or living it down.

Maybe all men are created equal, but somewhere along the line somebody checks your addition.

Sub culture: the mold that grows on hero sandwiches.

All the world's a stage and everybody wants to be behind the scenes.

It's good to make new friends . . . then you don't have to use the ones you already have quite so often.

When someone says they're behind you all the way, make sure it isn't to kick you in the pants.

Do you ever get the feeling that life is a test and you weren't given the textbook?

Some people climb the ladder of success, and some people slide down the banister of complacency.

If you're going to call somebody else's bluff, make sure you're not standing too close to the edge of it.

Do you ever feel that everyone else travels life's highway, while you're out of gas on a cul-de-sac?

Beware of the man on the move . . . he may just be going around in circles.

People who are waiting for their ship to come in should realize it takes more than one bag of wind to fill the sails.

Do you ever feel as if life is born anew for others each day and you're just the diaper service?

People who still want to find their place in the sun obviously haven't heard about the ozone layer.

Most people want to make something of themselves . . . other than a fool, that is.

Some people carve their way to success and others just chisel it.

People wouldn't need to save face if they didn't go around sticking it in other people's business.

You know you're a loser if people are always either putting you off or putting you on.

Some days life seems like a bike race—and you're on an exercycle.

There's a big difference between resting on your laurels and lying on your accomplishments.

Everyone wants to find their place in the sun . . . that's why California real estate prices keep rising.

Some people pursue endeavors that are right up their alley; others pursue things right down their gutter.

Just because the Constitution guarantees the pursuit of happiness doesn't mean you're going to catch it.

When people turn over a new leaf, it's usually to rake it into a pile and burn it with the others.

People who get around are seldom square.

It's easy to find someone to look up to if you're always sitting down.

Some restaurants are so awful they should just put the food directly into the doggie bags without serving it.

There are two kinds of people in the world: those who have dreams of being discovered, and those who have nightmares of being found out.

Some people want respect so badly they are willing to beg for it.

Some people have a wry wit and others have a whole-wheat wit.

On the other hand, give some people enough rope and they'll hang you.

Nowadays, the counterculture is people hanging out at luncheonettes.

Do you ever get the feeling it's a jungle out there and you're just a French poodle?

Some people are born leaders and others just hate standing in line.

Some people enjoy the fruits of their labor; others just get the vegetables.

When opportunity finally does knock, you'll probably be in the shower.

Boor: someone who holds up both ends of a conversation.

Beware of the man on the move. He might be going downhill.

Do you ever feel like life is a long, elegant banquet, and you're fast-food take-out in a paper sack?

For some people, living on the edge means dangling their legs in their private swimming pool.

If something's eating you, you're too low down on the food chain.

Some people are born leaders and some people are bin loaders.

UPST No. AD 0024414
C S T No. AD 5006179

(wheeler)

Bookshop
Phone : 624106

CASH MEMO

a. h. wheeler & co. ltd.

19, M.G. Marg, Allahabad - 211 001

No. 6294

Date 2019/96

Qty.	Particulars	Amount
1.	Today's Chuckle 2500 Crest One Arena	100 00
	E.&O.E.	100 00

100/12.   BOOKS ONCE SOLD SHALL NEITHER BE RETURNED NOR EXCHANGED.   For A.H. Wheeler & Co. Ltd.

As Dr. Frankenstein used to say, "Some things build character and some characters build things."

Two wrongs don't make a right, but three lefts will.

Grace: the ability to look the other way when the check arrives.

When social climbing, try not to use grappling hooks.

Compromise: an agreement wherein each party thinks the other got shafted.

Charity: the incredibly generous spirit that prompts us to donate something we were going to throw away anyhow.

Most people are like instant coffee: the minute they get in a little hot water, they dissolve.

Duty: that which you hate to do, but love to brag about.

When it comes to lighting the way to the future, some people are living in the Dark Ages.

Life is trial and error, unless you're an incompetent crook, in which case life is error and trial.

Experience is what allows us to keep messing up without blushing.

Hospitality: making your guests feel at home, when you wish that's where they'd go.

A real drip: someone who doesn't have sense enough to come in out of the rain.

Gossips know how to keep a secret . . . in circulation.

Everyone's guaranteed the right of free speech in this country . . . as long as nobody is forced to listen to them.

The main reason people want their ship to come in is pier pressure.

The Ku Klux Klan has decided to stop acting so backward. From now on they're marching in designer sheets.

If crime doesn't pay, why are all the drug dealers driving fancy cars?

Opportunity may knock, but you're not going to hear it if you're sleeping in the backyard hammock.

Experience: the sum total of all the things you didn't really want to know in the first place.

Los Angeles has one of the toughest jaywalking laws in America . . . one violation and they take away your shoes.

In California they're so progressive that they've stopped talking to plants and moved on to talking to vegetables.

Some people have photographic memories . . . underdeveloped and negative.

A bore is someone who, when passing by, you wish they would.

There are so many lousy drivers in Los Angeles that the police give out season tickets.

Grace: when you can put your best foot forward without stepping on any toes.

Do you ever feel like life is a car wash and you're going through it on a bicycle?

Some people are listed in Who's Who and some people are listed in What's That?

Royal flush: when kings get embarrassed.

Civilization hasn't progressed so far. After all, primitive man cooked out on a barbecue every night.

People all wrapped up in themselves make very small packages.

Humility is the ability to attract attention while looking modest.

People who don't act their age are still studying for the part.

The problem with being punctual is that nobody else is there to know the difference anyway.

Have you ever noticed that when you make a total fool of yourself, everyone wants to be your press agent?

Some people have a way about them that seems to say, "If I only have one life to live, let me live it as a jerk."

There must be such a thing as luck. How else do you explain the successes of your rivals?

It's funny how the people who go out to get fame usually end up getting a reputation along the way.

You can tell how much pull you have by the number of people willing to give you a push.

Did you hear about the guy who wanted to move up in the world, so he became a second-story man?

Crime doesn't pay, but it does provide free room and board if you're caught.

Gossip: aerobic talking.

Pomposity is the mother of pretention.

So many people are living life in the fast lane these days, you can't even get on the highway.

You know you're getting successful when you start getting abused by a better class of people.

Present tense: when you're nervous about whether they'll like your gift.

He who laughs last is the one who didn't get the joke until it was explained to him.

Most of us can keep our lives on track all right . . . if you don't mind riding in the caboose.

Cruel and unusual punishment: being a school bus driver.

It's really depressing when you wait for your ship to come in, and it turns out to be a rubber raft.

Little did our forefathers know that they opened up the wilderness so that we could open up the shopping malls.

For most of us, the light at the end of the tunnel is just another tollbooth.

Population density is getting to be a real problem . . . particularly the density from the neck up.

Brainstorm: when you get an idea that's all wet.

Who said Americans are lazy? They work their fingers to the bone . . . switching the TV remote control.

Some people let the grass grow under their feet and others get mower out of life.

Life may be a cabaret, but most of us are stuck at the hat-check counter.

He used to have a police record, until he bought the compact disc.

Did you ever notice, when most people want you to play ball, they expect you to play the outfield?

Do you ever feel like other people are making their mark in the world while you're only making smudges?

Did you ever notice how people who say they're so busy are never too busy to stop and talk about how busy they are?

Life is like a game of cards: by the time you learn how to play, you're already lost in the shuffle.

The art of conversation: smile while pretending to listen to what the other person's saying.

Best method to keep others from jumping down your throat: keep your mouth shut.

Gangsters' motto: "A penny saved is one less copper in circulation."

Just remember, you can become a prince and still look like a frog.

How come small talk is the only thing that comes out of big mouths?

If variety is the spice of life, most of us feel like we're on salt-free diets.

Rugged individualist: one who buys only unusual carpets.

Why is it the minute your ship comes in there's a dockworkers' strike?

Acquaintance: someone you know well enough to borrow from but not to lend to.

People who drink and drive are putting the quart before the hearse.

There's a new club: A.A.A.A.A. It's for people who are driven to drink.

CREATURE COMFORTS

You know somebody's painted the town red when that's the color of their eyes the next morning.

Some Chinese restaurants are completely automated now, and others still prefer to let their fingers do the wokking.

Energy crisis: when you can't fuel all of the people all of the time.

Used car: one that's not all it's jacked up to be.

Recliner chair: vinyl resting place.

Rule for eating in fancy restaurants: if you can't pronounce it, you can't afford it.

They say TV is still in its infancy, which is why you have to change it so often.

Sunday driving: the crawl of the open road.

Perfect gift for the man who has everything: a burglar alarm.

Modern appliances are great. In the old days you always had to pry the burnt toast out of the toaster. Now the burnt toast pops up all by itself.

Food processor: a device for cutting leftovers into smaller pieces before throwing them out.

Cover charge: electric blanket.

Summer on the Riviera: French fry.

For some people, meditating in the Lotus position means going out and buying a $60,000 sports car.

Freedom of the press: nonwrinkle clothes.

Did you hear about the waterbed sale where they were flooded with calls?

There's one good thing about nouvelle cuisine: no leftovers.

Ladies' footwear motto: "If the shoe fits, it's the wrong style."

Shopping motto: "If the shoe fits, charge it."

Watch dog: an ugly timepiece.

The ties that bind: lace-up shoes.

Aid to good digestion: beware of menus with too many exclamation points.

Picnic: snack in the grass.

If travel is a broadening experience, why do they keep making those airline seats smaller?

Maybe lite beer is so popular because you won't be as heavy to carry when you pass out.

Most nylon stockings give you a run for the money.

Slugfest: escargot cook-off.

If only people who are driven to drink were driven home again instead of driving themselves.

America's love affair with the car has degenerated into autoeroticism.

If the shoe fits, it's probably the most expensive one in the store.

Invoice for a new boat: bill of sail.

I don't know what the big attraction of piano bars is; who wants to see a bunch of drunken pianos?

You know you've had too much to drink when you get so carried away at a party that you get carried away at a party.

Electric bill: charge of the light brigade.

If people go on vacations for peace and quiet, why do they dress so loud?

Then there was the tourist in Idaho who was strictly a meet-the-potatoes man.

In Beverly Hills they have carpools, too. Those are cars with pools in them.

Some people love Chinese food so much they'll worship the ground you wok on.

Clearance sale on male footwear: these are the times to try men's soles.

Living in the lap of luxury is all right, except you never know when luxury is going to stand up.

Feedback: reciprocal lunches.

Travel broadens one . . . particularly if you eat in all those fancy restaurants.

If you really want to witness a lot of self-serving people, watch the line at a buffet table.

They say sloth is one of the seven deadly sins, but mink and ermine are more popular.

Car alarms are wonderful. They give thieves something to whistle along to while they hot-wire your ignition.

You know it's an informal dinner party when they've got recliner chairs around the dining-room table.

Once upon a time, a country club was nothing but a big stick in the woods.

Seafood restaurants are for people who feel like a fish out of water.

Most bar patrons like their drinks like roofs . . . on the house.

Mafia seafood restaurant: Mobsters and Lobsters.

Some supermarket shoppers have no shelf control.

Chef-school graffiti: "For a good thyme, call 555-9142."

If shopping centers get much bigger, the suburbs are going to have to move.

If you buy the wrong-size shoes, ignorance is blisters.

The last resort: what you're stuck with when you make your vacation plans late.

Buffet: where there's plenty of the kinds of food you don't like, and then there's no place to sit down.

When giving a gift, nothing beats the elegant simplicity of money.

Horn of plenty: the sound of a traffic jam.

The rich are different from you and me . . . their main exercise is raking in the dough.

What happens when there are too many cars: sins of emission.

Some people travel to forget . . . their razor, their tickets, their best tie . . .

What do they mean when they say someone drinks like a fish? Have you ever seen a drunken fish?

Modern furniture is obviously designed by people who prefer to stand.

Here's an alternative to the death penalty: let's make offenders work summers in amusement parks, dressed up in animal costumes.

If the Japanese don't want to buy cars from us, maybe we can at least get them to buy some of those fuzzy dice.

Some people say airlines serve dog food on their flights, but they're wrong. Dog food contains essential minerals and vitamins.

By the time you can afford a meal fit for a king, you need a food taster.

Exclusive club: one where they weigh your wallet at the door.

Sign outside a lousy restaurant: "Sorry, we're open."

Some wines should be opened so they can breathe . . . and others so they can gasp.

People change. And, hygienically speaking, we should all be grateful for that.

Dessert store on the endangered list: Custard's Last Stand.

Do you ever get the feeling that in this game of life, you're on the sidelines holding up the mascot's tail?

You know the saloon's a classic when the bar talk turns to Bartók.

Sleeping bag: nap sack.

When couch potatoes pause on the educational TV channel they have a near-depth experience.

People who drink too many spirits become a ghost of their former selves.

Things haven't improved much since Columbus's day. He set out for the Far East and wound up in the Caribbean. Now, when you go to the Far East you get there all right, but your luggage goes to the Caribbean.

How about that new restaurant they opened on the moon? Fabulous food, no atmosphere.

People in bars usually act so down-to-earth because they're freshly plowed.

Sign in a restaurant: "Eat now, pay waiter."

Nowadays, wine, women, and song cost so much that there's hardly anything left over for luxuries.

What happens if you can't pay your bill at a sidewalk café . . . do they throw you inside?

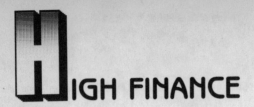

HIGH FINANCE

A good businessman is one who loses his shirt and then pretends he's going on a beach vacation.

Entrepreneur: someone who has the franchise for crutches at a ski resort.

Then there was the business conference where the speaker was so full of hot air everyone came out with blow-dried hair.

Finance: the art of passing money from hand to hand until it disappears.

Stock-market crash: when you go from having a corner on the market to having a market on the corner.

Noah was quite a financier: he floated his stock when everyone else was being liquidated.

The IRS has the perfect gift for the man who has everything: an audit.

The person who says they just blew a fortune in the market may have just come from the grocery store.

Bank: an institution that urges you to save part of what you earn, then lends you money so you can spend more than what you earn.

Wall Street has a lot of people who are really going places. The problem is, one of the places is prison.

Wall Street: the din of inequity.

The usual reason for a stock-market crash is that no one's in the cockpit.

There are times in your life when you should take stock of yourself . . . but who needs another penny stock?

From the looks of Wall Street, our business schools are turning out grads of greed.

Before big business stole the term, "hostile takeover" used to mean gunboat diplomacy.

Royal CPA: a count accountant.

When it comes to white-collar crime, it seems there's something fishy with the scales of justice.

Then there was the guy who wanted to learn about stock and the market, so he got a job unloading trucks at the grocery store.

Corporate yes-men have nodding in common.

If you work in the stock market, your March probably will come in a-lyin' and go out on the lamb.

Money's tight. Even ice-cream corporations are complaining about frozen assets.

Wall Street didn't invent stocks and bonds . . . the Salem witch trials did.

When the world really does go to the dogs, you can bet that big business will corner the market on dog biscuits.

Asking a stockbroker to invest for you is like asking a fox to watch your chickens.

Autobiography: Henry Ford's memoirs.

These savings-and-loan guys would have us believe that booty is in the eye of the beholder.

You can't read a book by its cover, but you can know a lot about a corporation by its Chapter 11.

The stock market doesn't care that we're skating on thin ice. It just means the price of ice will go up.

Those savings-and-loan guys evidently thought the secret of success was excess.

People judge you by the company you keep . . . unless you work on Wall Street, in which case they judge you by the company you raid.

What they call federal investigations of those who made windfalls on junk bonds: Scrutiny on the Bounty.

Money-market managers are fund-loving people.

Why do they call it Wall Street when it's always going through either the ceiling or the floor?

Stock-market report: the toothpaste business has gone down the tubes.

How can people say big corporations are greedy, when all they're trying to do is give us the business?

Prehistoric man was never able to anticipate a drop in the rock market.

There's nothing wrong with the economy's soaring, but not when the budget is a blimp.

Stock-market aerobics: when the computers exercise their options.

Millionaire: that's the air your million vanished into.

Those Wall Street sharpies must be fond of water sports, considering how many of them are being sent up the river these days.

Others may have felt the recession, but over at the dynamite factory business is booming.

In the business world the early bird gets the worm, too. But the bird is a vulture.

If this country is going to the dogs, then how come all the fat cats are doing so well?

The rich *are* different from you and me . . . they don't pay taxes.

American executives have found a new way to cut costs and be more patriotic. Now they only drink domestic champagne at lunch.

What you use to tie two Chinese ships together: junque bonds.

Old pirates never die . . . they just become presidents of savings-and-loan associations.

You'll never get to the top of the corporate ladder if it's all work and no ploy.

Business acumen: that's when you open a big and tall men's shop in Pygmy territory.

The only sure way to clean up in the stock market is to become a janitor on Wall Street.

With the economy the way it is now, New Orleans is thinking of changing the name of the French Quarter to the French Dime.

High finance is like billiards: the object is to fill your pockets without getting behind the eight ball.

Some people read self-help books, but on Wall Street they read help-yourself books.

Did you hear about the cannibal who wouldn't eat the millionaire because he was trying to give up rich foods?

Remember when board games were something you played at home on the coffee table, instead of something you did at work in the conference room?

With some corporations, "quality" is their middle name . . . the only problem is, "lousy" is their first name.

They keep raising the stakes on Wall Street, but that's nothing new . . . cattlemen have been raising steaks for years.

Animal stock market: buy sheep and sell deer.

Some of these corporate executives have so much drive that they should have their licenses revoked.

They can talk all they want about the bulls and bears . . . it's the weasels who do well on Wall Street.

Recession: when the economy is in recess . . . usually on the swing or the slide.

Wall Street is very hygienic. There, you either clean up or end up taking a bath.

Investment opportunity: the point at which a fool and his money are parted.

The reason corporations have so many vice presidents is that there's so much vice to contend with.

America's a great country. Where else could a corporate chief lose billions of dollars for his company and get a million-dollar bonus for it?

With modern finance, things are often touch and go. First they touch you for the money, then you wonder where it all goes.

When banks go out of business, do you have to give the toaster back?

Up in the mountains, when they talk about liquid assets, they're referring to moonshine.

If there really was anything to this supply-and-demand stuff, how come there's such an overabundance of free advice?

Asking a stockbroker if you should invest in the market is like asking a dog if it's hungry.

Conglomerates are judged by the companies they keep.

From now on, "S & L" will stand for "secrets and lies."

If you want to be in a business that deals in big figures, buy a health club.

Stockbrokers are modern magicians . . . they know how to make your money disappear.

Bank: a place that gives you all the free calendars you want, but chains down all the ballpoint pens that don't work.

America's a great country. Where else can you talk about hard times over a twenty-dollar steak?

Times have been tough on a lot of people. One Texan is so strapped that the phone in his Rolls-Royce is on a party line.

Executive: someone who talks football at the office and business at the game.

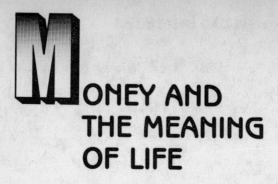

MONEY AND THE MEANING OF LIFE

What this country needs is a good five-cent nickel.

Never teach your kids the value of a dollar. They'll only want more.

You know you're in trouble when the strange noise coming from your car is the mechanic laughing underneath it.

Eat, drink, and be merry . . . as long as it's on your company expense account.

These days, the only way to make ends meet is if you're an accordion player.

There's nothing wrong with bringing home the bacon, but you don't have to become a pig in the process.

Wallets have gotten so expensive that if you buy one you won't have anything left to put in it.

Capitol gains: whenever you make money, the Capitol gains.

Running into debt: when you unexpectedly meet someone you owe money to.

A purse was designed so you can lose all your valuables at the same time.

Money goes as far as it ever did; it just goes a lot faster.

When your ship finally does come in, how come the IRS is on the dock unloading it?

Most of us wouldn't mind the rat race so much if we only could get a little more cheese.

It used to be a sin to be rich . . . now it's a miracle.

It's easier to start from scratch if you have some.

Inflation: that's when your kid starts his first job at a salary you dreamed would mark the pinnacle of your career.

Drive-in banking was invented so cars could see their real owners.

It's not wise to tell your kids the value of money anymore. You'll only discourage them.

How can you get ahead if you only work five days a week and spend money seven?

Optimist: someone who thinks he can live like a millionaire if he has a million dollars.

You know you're growing up when you still have ideals but you're willing to sell them for the right price.

Despite the cost of living, it's still popular.

Poverty is what we try to conceal while we're going through it and then brag about in our memoirs.

You know something's wrong when you start moonlighting to keep up the payments on all those labor-saving devices.

Some people cope with the bad economy by having yard sales . . . they sell their yards.

Always borrow from a pessimist. He doesn't think you're going to pay him back anyway.

Bill collectors always call at the most inopportune time . . . like when you're at home.

If food prices keep rising, politicians won't be the only ones sitting down to $100-a-plate dinners.

Paying your taxes goes for a good cause . . . it keeps you out of prison.

People aren't concerned that a dollar doesn't go as far as it used to; they're worried that it never stays put.

America is a land of untold wealth . . . just ask the IRS.

Ten cents used to be a lot of money. How dimes have changed.

Relative obscurity: when you have so little money that your relatives ignore you.

There's one good thing about living in the past . . . it's cheaper.

A loaf of bread, a jug of wine, and you've shot your weekly food budget.

Many an optimist has become rich by buying out a pessimist.

Fixed income: what's left after you've fixed the washing machine, the TV, the car, and the kid's bike.

If you don't think appearances are deceiving, keep in mind that a dollar looks the same as it did ten years ago.

Build a better mousetrap, and some rat will try to copy it.

By the time you pay all your bills each month, about the only thing left to spend is a nice, quiet evening at home.

The difference between a taxidermist and a tax collector is the taxidermist leaves the hide.

Most folks' financial problems are really quite simple . . . they don't have money.

Prosperity: that period between the last installment and the next purchase.

The way some people hold on to money, you'd think it was worth the paper it's printed on.

So what if our forefathers had to haul water from the well? At least they didn't have to stay up nights trying to figure out how to pay for the bucket.

Revolving credit: when you have to make a payment every time you turn around.

Most loans are usurer-friendly.

There are some things money just can't buy. Some stores in Beverly Hills demand gold bullion.

If money is the root of all evil, then credit cards must be the plant food.

The meek may inherit the earth, but it will be the pushy ones who'll hold all the mortgages.

Everybody wants their ship to come in, but not many are willing to swim out and tow it to shore.

Why is it that the less bread you make, the more dough you need?

If money talks, then why is silence golden?

If you really want to be a breadwinner, maybe you should enter a bakery sweepstakes.

Old gold diggers are like trees: you can tell their age by counting the rings.

Banker comedian: credit card.

The only way you get to be toast of the town is by having a lot of bread.

Some people seek the key to success and others just seek the lockpick.

Making buckskin jackets may not pay much, but there are fringe benefits.

Money may be the root of all evil, but greed is the fertilizer.

What's the point in trying to save for a rainy day if they keep raising the price of umbrellas?

Why do people complain about cash-flow problems? It's really very simple . . . you get some cash and out it flows.

The nicest gift is always something you made yourself . . . like money, for instance.

Many a dreamboat has sailed right through someone else's liquid assets.

Why do they call it "price fixing" when it always "breaks" the consumer?

If you think money grows on trees, just try paying for something with a bunch of leaves.

How come when something tickles your fancy it usually beats up your pocketbook?

If people are really concerned about conserving water, maybe criminals should cut down on laundering money.

For some stingy people, the last will becomes the last won't.

Last will and testament: where you heir your differences.

Money talks, but if you think it listens, just try getting a loan.

The economy finally caught up with the foundation-garment industry. Everything went bust.

Will power: the ability to make your heirs behave by threatening to cut them out of it.

If you overcharge on your credit cards, maybe it's time for some plastic surgery.

It used to be we couldn't see the forest for the trees. Now we can't see the forest for all the shopping malls.

Spend each day as if it were your last . . . and you'll be broke by sunset.

How come every sales pitch is either a fastball or a curve?

There's a new incentive program that a few corporations are trying out. It's called a decent paycheck.

Ancient fishing villages used to barter with fish instead of using money. They were the first to use credit cods.

Most people don't really want to make money . . . they want to collect it.

Did you hear about the two guys who stopped writing when they became pen pals? They went to the same prison for passing bad checks.

Some people can make ends meet . . . and for others the ends can only wave from a distance.

A checkbook is a funny thing: once you've started it, it's hard to put it down until you've finished it.

Not all people sell out. Some lease with an option to buy.

Some people think that the best way to stretch your money is to write rubber checks.

You might as well get a grip on yourself . . . all your creditors have one on you.

Sure, you can be poor and happy . . . just not at the same time.

Some people have their feet planted firmly in the ground . . . and others just move like it.

Did you hear about the barbecue store that was having a fire sale?

Of course money doesn't buy happiness, but long-term leases are available.

By the time the baby boomers are ready to collect their Social Security checks, "the golden years" will turn into "the tin years."

Spendthrift: someone who thinks a nest egg is for the birds.

Some banking customers treat their withdrawal slips like take-out menus.

If money doesn't grow on trees, why are so many people willing to put themselves out on a limb for it?

The difference between cheating the IRS and crossing a street in New York City: one is tax evasion and the other is taxi evasion.

Fund-raising party: a fete worse than death.

By the time you get to the end of the rainbow, the pot of gold will have become a bushel basket of promissory notes.

The IRS already knows that every cloud has a silver lining.

Have you ever noticed that a lot of people who make the most bread are the biggest crumbs?

Lots of people are go-getters. The problem is getting them to bring it back.

Trying to balance a budget is like a game of pool: you're behind the eight ball and all you see are a bunch of open pockets.

They call it branch banking because of all the people who've put themselves out on a financial limb.

Show me someone who's spent all their inheritance and I'll show you someone who doesn't have the cents they were born with.

There's no point in looking for the key to success. They're using combination locks now.

Most people live by the golden rule: he who has the most gold, rules.

The world is your oyster . . . but only if you have enough clams.

These days, the only time the buck stops anywhere is to be laundered.

The problem with a pitch is there's usually a catch.

People who say money's no object usually mean it's no object they can get ahold of.

Money mad: dough nut.

You usually know someone has a lot of lettuce by their dressing.

Money may be the root of all evil, but most of us just want to shake the branches a little.

Inheritance: the most popular labor-saving device.

Some people are self-made, and others are store-bought on credit.

Money talks: it says good-bye.

The minute you make ends meet, they say good-bye again.

The only thing dirt cheap anymore is dirt.

Most people work like dogs so they can live in nicer kennels.

They say money doesn't go as far as it used to, but it certainly isn't getting any closer.

It's easy to make a fortune in Vegas . . . but only if you own the casino.

Money won't buy friends, but it sure makes for some enthusiastic acquaintances.

The IRS sure knows how to take our money. You've really got to hand it to them.

There's no shame in being poor. It's just that, in this day and age, who can afford it?

The first guy to make a mountain out of a molehill probably worked for the IRS.

How come the minute you have money to burn, the government buys a new incinerator?

Most people don't mind working for a good cause . . . like a new set of golf clubs.

The first praise was invented by someone who wanted a raise.

Money may not buy happiness, but at least it keeps your family from ignoring you altogether.

Experience: when we brag about past endeavors that didn't make a dime.

Show me someone who falls down on the job and I'll show you an insurance scam.

If you have money to burn, there will always be some opportunist to offer you a match.

The difference between a luxury and a necessity is directly proportional to your inability to pay for it.

They say money talks, but most of us only hear it laughing as it goes by.

First line of the Las Vegas town charter: "A fool and his money are soon parted."

Time is money . . . at least that's what the credit-card companies believe.

Last will: "Being of sound mind, I spent it on chorus girls."

Nostalgia is the ability to remember yesterday's prices while forgetting yesterday's wages.

Extravagance: the foolish spending habits of someone else, which you wish you could afford to emulate.

People who complain about the high cost of living should check out funeral prices these days.

If you really want to improve your station in life, go to work for the railroad.

Some people run into debt, and others buy flashy new cars and drive into it in style.

Collecting is a great hobby. Maybe you should try it with money sometime.

These days, by the time your ship comes in, you've already retired to the desert.

Put your money where your mouth is . . . eat your wallet.

Life has gotten so expensive. Just make one claim on your life insurance and your premiums go up.

Whoever said "better late than never" was obviously never audited.

Car sickness: that feeling you get every month when the payment is due.

Money might as well grow on trees, the way it always leaves.

Price ceilings are back . . . when you hear the price you hit the ceiling.

Recession: when the amenities are beyond your meanities, and the niceties have such high priceties.

Banks now offer split-level deposit boxes for the very rich.

Money won't buy happiness, but it does allow you to rent an awful lot of distractions along the way.

Blood may be thicker than water, but it's still thinner than money.

The best things in life may not be free, but up until now at least they've been tax-deductible.

It's called take-home pay because that's the only place you can afford to go with it.

There are a lot of things in life more important than money, but it takes money to buy them.

Did it ever occur to you that the reason Robin Hood robbed only from the rich is that the poor have no money?

The IRS is helping us all with our errands this year . . . by taking us to the cleaners.

Money is one of those rare things where quantity does equal quality.

Motto least likely to be seen at the IRS office: "Money isn't everything."

Surefire money-making scheme: get a job.

Never put off until tomorrow what you can do today . . . there will only be a higher tax on it.

So what if money talks? It's impossible to hold on to it long enough to have a conversation.

Most of us don't mind paying as we go. It's paying where we've been that's the problem.

It's easier to meet your expenses than it is to say good-bye to them.

Thanks to automatic teller machines, you're always conveniently close to being broke.

You've probably noticed that when money talks nobody corrects its grammar.

Motto of the IRS: "Success has its price."

If a man cannot live by bread alone, it's probably because he lacks the dough.

Joint checking: when your local bar cashes them for you.

A person can be successful and honest . . . just not at the same time.

Inflation: when all your liquid assets go down the drain.

Everyone should try to save some money. Economic experts claim it will be worth something again someday.

The only way some people can be paid what they're worth is if they abolish the minimum-wage law.

Inflation: the art of cutting a dollar in half without touching the paper.

The surest way to make ends meet is to get off your own.

The only reason some people can keep their heads above water is that wood floats.

Money may not be everything, but it does keep you in touch with your children.

Inflation: the system whereby if you save long enough to buy something, you can't afford it.

Whoever said money doesn't buy happiness has never done much shopping.

LIFE'S INSTRUCTIONS

Whoever said you can't take it with you has obviously never traveled in a camper.

Most people who sow their wild oats take them fermented.

Most people don't open the door when opportunity knocks because they're afraid of catching a draft.

Confidence: the ability to be wrong with absolute conviction.

About the only way to get people to pay attention anymore is to issue them receipts.

If practice made perfect, everyone would know how to be a good loser.

If at first you don't succeed, you've got a lot of company.

If first impressions are lasting impressions, who figured out how to eat an artichoke?

Life is unpredictable . . . just ask anyone who ever bet on a sure thing.

A boor is someone who is successful in the endeavor you failed at.

The meek will inherit the earth, but give them a few weeks with it and they'll be just as pushy as the rest of us.

If people are constantly stringing you along, you're a real yo-yo.

Whoever advised not to cry over spilt milk obviously hasn't bought any lately.

Nobody ever told us that the straight and narrow path had so many potholes.

Advice: a conversation in which your eyes glaze over and your ears stop up.

The hardest part about finding greener pastures is all the bull you encounter.

If you have what it takes, there'll always be someone ready to take it.

If you learn a new word every day and use it, in no time you'll be completely incomprehensible to others.

By the time the meek inherit the earth, our inheritance will have been squandered.

Experience: what you think you have until you get more.

It's a small world . . . once you've finally made it to the airport.

If you think one person can't make a difference in this world, consider the lone cigar smoker in a restaurant.

You can't fool all of the people all of the time . . . unless you design highway interchanges.

Always remember, a day without sunshine is like night.

If you really want somebody to get what's coming to them, don't mail it.

If you make a better lawn, the world will beat a path across it to your door.

Just remember, these are the good old days you're going to miss twenty years from now.

If you ask enough people for advice, you can eventually find someone who will tell you to do what you were going to do anyway.

Never be nostalgic about anything unless there's absolutely no chance of its coming back again.

Don't worry about finding your station in life. Somebody will tell you where to get off.

Just remember: today's headlines are wrapped around tomorrow's garbage.

Everyone has a little of the milk of human kindness, but they usually put it in the coffee of cynicism.

Life's lessons could be learned much more quickly if they'd quit assigning homework.

It used to be that a sense of honor would see you through . . . now only a sense of humor will do it.

There comes a time when you have to put your foot down. After all, keeping it in your mouth constantly will wrinkle your toes.

Life is sweet on the sunny side of the street, but only if you've got on sunblocker #16.

Shakespeare said, "Life is but a dream," but, if that's true, who wants a wake-up call?

There's nothing wrong with persistence . . . if you give it a rest once in a while.

You don't really know someone until you walk a mile in their shoes . . . and by then you're too far away to get acquainted.

We wouldn't mind traveling the highway of life so much if we didn't have to keep paying tolls.

Most people miss their calling because they can't hear it over their complaining.

If you don't mind your manners, it's a sure thing that somebody will.

It seems like you spend all your time either trying to buckle down or zip up.

Inside every one of us there's a child yearning to get out . . . and, unfortunately, he usually does.

Life is a journey in which most of us get travel sickness.

Boys will be boys . . . for much longer than is generally necessary.

What would have happened at the dawn of civilization if they'd been wearing sunglasses?

An optimist thinks the glass is half full; a pessimist thinks the glass is half empty. A realist knows that if he sticks around, he's eventually going to have to wash the glass.

Let the meek inherit the earth; they can keep up the payments for a while.

No man's an island . . . it wouldn't be atoll proper.

Just because there are other fish in the sea doesn't mean you can get one to nibble your line.

Whoever said talk is cheap never dialed one of those 900 phone numbers.

If you've lost your memory, forget about it.

Blessed are the meek . . . they always get out of the way before you have to push them.

Maybe the milk of human kindness would flow more freely if someone brought the cookies of compassion.

Some people look before they leap, and others spy before they slither.

Two generic items we'd like to see: common sense and plain English.

Ask not for whom the bell tolls. Nobody will be able to hear you with all that racket, anyway.

Virtue may be its own reward, but then, so is vice.

Into every life some rain must fall, but some people install their own sprinkler systems.

People used to just look for the free lunch . . . now they want it delivered, too.

They say rock and roll will never die, but it's certainly having an unattractive old age.

It's hard to stand on your own two feet if you're always putting them in your mouth.

The problem with living life in the fast lane is that they never tell you the price of gas beforehand.

Some funeral parlors are so tacky, you wouldn't want to be caught dead in one.

All things come to those who wait, but by then, you've forgotten what you wanted in the first place.

When someone calls you "the salt of the earth," they're probably preparing to treat you like dirt.

Lots of people live life on the edge . . . on the edge of the couch.

There's nothing wrong with being misunderstood. Who wants others to know what you're thinking anyway?

Usually the only way to get a spark of inspiration is from the bonfire of frustration.

Experience: what you get instead of what you were going after.

The best part about telling the truth is that you don't have to remember what you said.

You should learn to laugh at yourself. After all, everybody else has been doing it for some time.

The best way to keep your chin up is to close your mouth and quit complaining.

Experience is that which allows us to be stupid in totally original ways.

Punctuality: the desire to punch out the person who's late for your appointment.

If at first you don't succeed, no one will be surprised.

The secret of success is to always have the answers . . . even if you have to make them up.

The easiest way to be a man of few words is to always respond, "I understand perfectly."

Just when everything seems to be going your way, you realize it's other people chasing you.

If people really profited from their mistakes, we'd all be rich by now.

It's all right to have people eating out of your hand . . . as long as they don't slobber.

The world may be your oyster, but that doesn't mean you can spend your time in dives.

Man cannot live by bread alone. That's why he's always getting in some kind of jam.

If nothing is impossible, then how come you can't pick up a magazine without one of those subscription postcards falling out?

Eat, drink, and be merry . . . and you'll become a silly, overweight alcoholic.

If you want other people to dance to your tune, don't play it on the bagpipes.

Beware of people who worship the ground you walk on . . . they may just be reaching for some dirt.

We don't learn from our mistakes nearly as much as we learn by getting caught at them.

Human character is like a soufflé: you don't know until the last minute if it will rise to the occasion.

As you go down life's highway, you can't help but notice the traffic jam on the exit to easy street.

It's a lot easier to get people to sing your praises than to dance to your tune.

Go out and make your mark in the world, but try to avoid using a stubby crayon.

The best way to turn over a new leaf is by raking up the old ones in a pile and burning them.

It's easy to forgive and forget . . . just not at the same time.

People who get carried away with themselves usually have to walk back alone.

When someone wants you to follow their train of thought, make sure they don't have a loco motive.

The hardest part about climbing the ladder of success is climbing over all the people sleeping at the bottom.

Never make the same mistake twice, or you'll never get around to making them all.

The shortest distance between two points is usually between someone's ears.

Lots of people will give you the shirt off their back . . . if you invite them to your swimming pool.

You know you've given too long a speech when the audience engages in group snoring.

Lack of tact: the ability to put your foot in your mouth and step on somebody's toes at the same time.

Have you noticed that all the wrong people have inferiority complexes?

As soon as you learn to stand on your own two feet, somebody ties your shoelaces together.

If at first you don't succeed, pass the job on to your secretary.

There wouldn't be a rat race if there were enough cheese to go around.

Confidence is that glow you feel before you fail.

The best way to get a swelled head is to let a lot of people pump you full of hot air.

The grass on the other side of the fence might be greener because it's Astroturf.

Things usually go to pot because people fly off the handle when things don't immediately pan out.

If at first you don't succeed, try to pass the blame.

Since living well is almost impossible these days, more people are finding that revenge is the best revenge.

There's nothing wrong with lending a helping hand . . . the problem is getting people to let go of it.

If you want to know the definition of the term "fair-weather friends," just move to the beach.

Good judgment comes from experience. Experience comes from lousy judgment.

If all the world's a stage, how come none of us ever get the parts we audition for?

If people would build bridges instead of fences, they could charge tolls.

It's easy to find the key to success. The hard part is finding which door it opens.

Opportunity has to knock, but all temptation has to do is stand outside and whistle.

Lots of people can use their heads, but the part they use is mainly the mouth.

It's one thing to be guided by the hand of fate, but why does it always have to be balled up in a fist?

As the twig is bent, so grows the tree. That's why there are so many big saps.

When the going gets tough, the tough get going. The question is, where do they run off to?

Everyone has to have standards, but if you set them low enough, they're not hard to live up to.

The best way to make a long story short is to interrupt.

Public speaking is the art of turning a short subject into a full-length feature.

The best way to make a long story short is to tell the truth instead.

Lack of decisiveness is probably a bad trait . . . on the other hand, maybe not.

People who live in glass houses are all looking for maids who do windows.

Nobody ever told us the highway of life was a toll road.

Always remember: there's a difference between getting a second wind and being full of hot air.

Don't take it too seriously when your name comes up . . . it'll always come down again.

If you drive recklessly down life's highway, you're sure to reach your final destination more quickly.

You start out thinking you have a spark of genius and end up just having plenty of gas.

How can you be an upright citizen with your shoulder to the wheel and your nose to the grindstone?

What this country needs is some cheap ice to go along with all the cheapskates.

When things start going your way, it's usually because you stopped going the wrong way down a one-way street.

To the victor goes the spoils . . . but who wants it if it's spoiled?

You know you've really hit on something when the lump forms on your head.

It's not how you play the game of life . . . it's who's holding the dice.

People who think they have a lot going for them usually have something coming to them.

People who think they have what it takes usually get taken.

People who burn their bridges behind them must be collecting fire insurance.

Life is always a lot of give-and-take. If you can take it, there's always somebody willing to give it out.

Some kinds of people come along only once in a generation . . . and that's often enough.

Irony: when you've saved for a rainy day and get transferred to Nevada.

People used to do things by the book because people used to read books.

Ever since man discovered fire there's always been someone who'll make an ash of himself.

Never trust anyone who will sell out and takes credit cards.

Give some people an inch, and they'll call the surveyor.

The only problem with trying to bury your past is that you'll usually get a little dirt on yourself in the process.

Life is a lot like bowling . . . no sooner do you get on a roll than you wind up in the gutter.

It's the little things in life that bring happiness . . . provided, of course, that you can't get your hands on the big things.

The reason most folks don't show any horse sense is that they don't want to be saddled with responsibility.

Compromise: the art of all parties giving up a little until everyone's dissatisfied.

A friend in need laughs at all your jokes.

As you sail through life, remember this: you're either going up the creek or down the river.

Whenever driving a point home, it's best to look at it by the porch light before taking it inside.

Maybe you can't take it with you, but if you spend it now you can keep others from taking it with them after they've taken you away.

When people say don't ever change, they mean don't do it in front of open windows.

You shouldn't hold a grudge for too long. After all, you can always pick it up again.

If life is really a test of some sort, let's vote to have it graded on a curve.

Integrity is a valuable thing; that's why people are willing to pay so handsomely for it.

Some people need to be handled with kid gloves . . . and some people need to be handled with kid mittens and mitten clips.

Life is a journey. It's just that some take the highway while the rest of us discover all the dead ends.

It's all right to put your best foot forward . . . just watch where you step.

It used to be you had to walk a mile in someone else's shoes to know how they felt. Now you have to drive around the beltway in their car.

Life isn't a dress rehearsal . . . which is a good thing, because nobody seems to know their lines.

If you can keep your head when those about you are losing theirs, you're probably the guy operating the guillotine.

Man does not live by bread alone. He needs buttering up occasionally.

If you build a better mousetrap, you'll have to join the rat race in order to sell it.

Whoever said you can't get something for nothing has obviously never received junk mail.

Sound idea: one that only sounds good.

Next time you're feeling sorry for yourself, just be thankful you don't have to wear lederhosen.

The best way to get ahead in this world is to grow one on your neck.

Don't ever put someone else on a pedestal . . . they're in too good a position to throw things at you.

As you play the game of life, remember: it's not who has more on the ball . . . it's who has the better racket.

If you're always waiting for the right thing, you may end up with whatever's left.

Manhood begins by trying to shave face and ends by trying to save face.

We have seen the future, and it is expensive.

Everybody has mountains they must climb . . . except the rich, who simply charter jets.

Today is the first day of the rest of your life. Now you can start messing up all over again.

Into each life some rain must fall . . . usually just about the time you get to the beach.

History repeats itself, but it keeps getting more expensive.

Lots of people will take no for an answer . . . if you repeat it four or five times.

Perfection is the ability to mess up when there are no witnesses.

Beware of the self-made man. He may be looking for a construction improvement loan.

Anyone who offers you pie in the sky is likely to deliver pie in the face.

If you're the strong, silent type, people might mistake you for a lawn ornament.

These days the only time you put somebody on a pedestal is if you need them to change a light bulb.

Maturity is whether you can draw your own conclusions or just scribble them.

Save your money for a rainy day . . . then invest in umbrellas.

The best way to be unpopular is to set a good example.

Most people don't know what they really want . . . they just know they haven't got it yet.

Never put off until tomorrow what you can do today . . . unless you've already made your full quota of mistakes.

Graciousness is the ability to be nice to those who are of no possible use to you.

For some people life is at a crossroads; for others it's just happy trails.

Insistence: when persistence meets resistance.

Nobody likes a wise guy . . . particularly one who's right.

There are always two sides to every issue: the winning side and the losing side.

The fastest way to get behind the eight ball is to take the wrong cue.

If at first you don't succeed, at least you'll get lots of free advice on how to.

What most people need is more horsepower and less exhaust.

Beware of those who bow before you. They're probably just reaching for a corner of the rug.

Never kick someone when they're down . . . unless you're sure they can't get up again.

THE LAST WORD

Most people think the best way to have the last word is to string a whole bunch of other ones in front of it.

Many a last word became the first word of an argument.

We've all written letters we've later regretted sending, but at least there's comfort in knowing they'll only arrive long after anyone cares.

If you want to have the last word, make it "good-bye."

If you *really* want the last word, say "zymurgy."

ABOUT THE AUTHOR

"Today's Chuckle" was created in 1948 by Tom Collins, the former executive editor of the *Chicago Daily News*. Carrying on the family tradition, Harlan Collins now edits the feature, which appears in more than fifty papers across the country through the Los Angeles Times Syndicate. Harlan Collins lives in Nashville, Tennessee.

Elizabeth.